A PRACTICAL GUIDE TO

Organization Design

Margaret R. Davis, Ph.D. and David A. Weckler, Ph.D.

CRISP.
Learning

Menlo Park, California

A PRACTICAL GUIDE TO
Organization Design

Margaret R. Davis, Ph.D.
David A. Weckler, Ph.D.

CREDITS:
Managing Editor: **Kathleen Barcos**
Editor: **Janis Paris**
Designer: **ExecuStaff**
Typesetting: **ExecuStaff**
Cover Design: **London Road Design**

© 1996 by Crisp Publications, Inc.
Printed in the United States of America by Von Hoffmann Graphics, Inc.

CrispLearning.com

00 01 02 03   10 9 8 7 6 5 4 3

Library of Congress Catalog Card Number 95-83228
Organization Design
Davis, Ph.D., Margaret and Weckler, Ph.D., David
ISBN-1-56052-388-3

Dedication

To Ray, with love, for his infinite patience and helpful ideas; to Janet and Bert for their loving support; and to Robert and Elaine, my computer experts.

M.R.D.

To Barbara and Lily, with love and appreciation for their support and encouragement.

D.A.W.

CONTENTS

INTRODUCTION
1

Chapter One

FIRST STEPS
9

Chapter Two

DIVIDING UP THE WORK
25

Chapter Three

MANAGEMENT STRUCTURE
57

Chapter Four

COORDINATION AND CONTROL
87

Chapter Five

MEASURING PERFORMANCE
113

Chapter Six

PUTTING THE PIECES TOGETHER
127

REFERENCES AND FURTHER READING
139

GLOSSARY
143

ABOUT THE AUTHORS
153

INTRODUCTION

This book is about organization design. *Organization design* is the planning and fitting together of the people and activities involved in doing the work of an organization. It includes creating the "boxes and lines" of an organization chart and finding ways to make sure that the right work gets done the right way—with the desired results.

An *organization* is any collection of people and activities formed for a specific purpose. The world we interact with every day is filled with organizations of all kinds: product manufacturers, retail stores, banks, government agencies, volunteer associations. And there are organizations within organizations: General Motors is an organization, and so are the divisions that produce Chevrolets, Pontiacs, Buicks, Cadillacs. Each department within each division is an "organization within an organization."

This book was written for anyone who is embarking on the design or redesign of an organization. The ideas and techniques we present can be used in any organization: large and small; profit and nonprofit; public and private; industrial, professional, government and educational. We give examples and exercises to help you apply the ideas to your own organization.

If you follow management trends in the news media, you will know that new buzzwords appear at frequent intervals. For example, in recent years, we have heard much about "reengineering," "teams," "rightsizing," "total quality management," "business process improvement," and so on. Many of these approaches add valuable new perspectives to the business of organization design. But to make any of them work you need to understand the basics of organization design as we present them here.

Meaning of Words We Use

A glossary at the end of the book defines all the terms we use. For now, you need to understand our particular usage of a few key words.

An **organization** is any collection of people and activities formed for a specific purpose. We use the words *organization, business, company, corporation, enterprise* and *firm* more or less interchangeably. We do this simply to avoid being repetitive. These ideas apply no matter what kind of organization you have.

Unit is a generic term used to describe any subdivision of an organization. Divisions, departments, sections, work groups and teams are all units.

Customer means "anyone who uses the products or services you provide." In your business, these people might be called *clients* or *users,* for example, rather than customers.

Stakeholders are all those people or institutions who have an interest in your organization and who can influence what you do and how successful you are. For a typical business, stakeholders include owners, employees, customers, shareholders, suppliers, regulators and even competitors.

WHY DOES ORGANIZATION DESIGN MATTER?

Although it is true that the unique personalities of individuals in an organization influence everything that goes on, it is also true that the "impersonal" design factors we discuss here have a very powerful impact on shaping people's attitudes and behavior and on their opportunities and performance on the job. A good design greatly enhances organizational effectiveness; a poor design can, and often does, actively prevent the organization from being successful.

This brings to mind a dilemma that people often face when they set out to redesign an organization. This is, to what extent should you focus on building an "ideal" organization rather than creating a design that fits the employees and facilities already in place? We suggest you (1) think through what an "ideal" organization design would be, (2) see how this fits with your existing resources and (3) do some tweaking to both the design and the people to get a satisfactory resolution. Even if the immediate compromise is a long way from the "ideal," you will have some ideas as to what to aim for in the long run.

PUTTING ORGANIZATION DESIGN IN CONTEXT

It is worth noting that organization design is one of four steps in organizing or reorganizing a business enterprise. The four steps are:

1. **Assessing the Business Situation**
   - Opportunities and Threats
   - Resources

2. **Developing a Business Strategy**
   - Mission, Goals
   - Key Success Factors
   - Customer Needs
   - Products, Services

3. **Organization Design**
   - Business Processes
   - Dividing up the Work
   - Management Structure
   - Coordination, Control, Measurement

4. **Implementing the New Design**
   - Ongoing Monitoring of Design Effectiveness

The first step, *assessing the business situation,* consists of scanning the business environment, noting what opportunities and threats exist for the organization, and what resources are available, or need to be obtained, to compete. Together, these assessments influence the perceived need to change.

This leads to the second step, *developing a business strategy.* This includes reviewing the organization's mission, setting goals, defining key success factors, determining customer needs and products and services to offer. Although not the subject of this book, we briefly discuss mission, goals, and success factors in the next chapter because the chances of designing an effective organization are greater if these issues are clear.

Third, there is the topic of this book, *organization design.* This step includes describing business processes; deciding how best to split up people and work into units like divisions, departments and teams; creating a management structure and finding ways to coordinate and control work and to measure results.

Fourth, *implementation* is when the new design is put into operation. This is not as final a step as it sounds. In most companies, organization design is an ongoing process with much rethinking, tweaking and modifying of current arrangements.

WHEN DO YOU NEED TO REDESIGN AN ORGANIZATION?

The purpose of organization design is to help the organization use its resources in the best way possible to reach its goals and carry out its business strategies. It is appropriate to revisit the way your organization is designed whenever:

◇ Your organization is faced with an immediate or anticipated change in its situation—for example, new competition, new markets, new products or services, major changes in technology, a merger with another company—anything that results in new goals and new business strategies.

◇ For any reason you feel the need to improve organizational performance—for example, to reduce costs, increase profitability or improve quality.

The old adage, "if it ain't broke, don't fix it," can be highly misleading in today's business world. Technological breakthroughs occur frequently, spread quickly and can dramatically shift your formula for success. New opportunities that arise often give you only a brief window of time to react before the competition beats you to it.

Successful companies today are constantly responding to any changes they see coming up—in business opportunities, technology, resources, competition, regulation or in anything that might affect their business. In fact, it has been said of Hewlett-Packard that they don't wait for a competitor to come out with a better product; instead, they make their own products obsolete *before* their competitors do.

At the same time, major organization redesigns can be costly, time consuming and demoralizing to employees—at least, in the short run. Changing the organization around just for the sake of it is unlikely to bring many benefits. What is beneficial is to make sure on an ongoing basis that your structure and management methods are helping, not hindering, the organization's success.

OBJECTIVES OF THIS BOOK

In writing this book, we have three aims: *first,* to summarize and simplify existing knowledge about organization design—that is, the rationale for alternative ways of doing things and the strengths and drawbacks of each alternative; *second,* to provide clear guidelines and questions to enable you to apply the ideas to your own case and, *third,* to do both these things in a way that is useful not only to managers but to everyone in an organization who may take part in a design process.

Today, more than ever before, employees at all levels are being drawn into task forces, teams, problem-solving groups and other situations where they are asked to give their opinions and help their organizations be more competitive. This book can help everyone make useful contributions.

QUESTIONS TO ASK BEFORE GETTING STARTED

You may be designing a brand-new organization, revamping an existing one or just making some minor changes in a few areas.

Whatever the scope of the design activity, it helps to be as clear as possible on five things.

1. *What are you setting out to do through organization design?* Is it a complete overhaul of your structure or of just one part, streamlining to cut costs, taking advantage of new technology, improving responsiveness to customers? Being clear on what you're trying to accomplish will help you focus on the right issues, choose the right people to involve and not wander off on tangents.

2. *How will you know when you have succeeded?* How do you plan to measure success? Through improved customer satisfaction ratings? Fewer product rejects? Less waste? Lower production costs? Reduced headcount? If you know what success is for you, you'll make better decisions throughout the design process.

3. *What stakeholders do you need to satisfy?* How will your key stakeholders be affected by changes you make in the organization? How can you make changes as easy as possible for them to accept? Keeping these things in mind as you go forward will help prevent confused or negative reactions afterwards.

4. *What resources do you have?* Your resources include employees—their numbers, skills, experience, knowledge. Resources also include time, money, materials, equipment, facilities and other people or sources of information and help outside your organization that are available to you.

5. *What barriers or constraints do you face?* A shortage of important resources is one constraint. Others may include laws and government regulations that affect your business, competition, labor union agreements that restrict the kind of work your employees can do, or reluctance to change of organizational members.

SYNOPSIS OF EACH CHAPTER

1. FIRST STEPS

What are mission, goals and key success factors? What are business processes and why is it important to understand yours?

This chapter briefly reviews mission, goals and key success factors. We then describe business processes and why they are important and give guidelines on how to define your own.

2. DIVIDING UP THE WORK: ORGANIZATION STRUCTURE

How can work best be divided into clusters of tasks and responsibilities? What are the relative merits and drawbacks of different ways of doing this?

We describe five ways of splitting up work: by function (for example, sales, manufacturing, accounting), by product or service, by type of customer or market, by business process or in a matrix form. We also describe which approach works best under what circumstances.

3. MANAGEMENT STRUCTURE

How many levels of supervision or management do you need? How many people should each supervisor oversee (span of control)? Should decisions be centralized or decentralized?

Your management structure directly affects management costs, communication, employee motivation, coordination and control and other factors. We point out what needs to be taken into account in designing management structure.

4. COORDINATION AND CONTROL

What methods should be used to coordinate the activities of different people and groups and to make sure the proper quantity and quality of work get done?

Coordination means pulling together people's work efforts to reach common goals: a product, a service, a satisfied customer. Control means making sure work is done correctly. We describe four techniques for coordinating and controlling work.

5. PERFORMANCE MEASUREMENT

Are you getting the results you want? If not, where and how do corrections need to be made?

People pay attention to what is measured. We discuss the basic steps in performance measurement, aspects of performance that are most commonly measured and some measurement pitfalls.

6. PUTTING THE PIECES TOGETHER

How does it all go together? What are critical aspects of implementing a new organization design?

We briefly discuss three major aspects of implementation: communication, impact analysis and transition management. We then review and summarize the major organization design issues we have presented.

Chapter One

FIRST STEPS

Before embarking on organization design, you must first understand where your organization is headed—in other words, your mission and goals—and what key factors are required for your success.

In this chapter, we discuss *mission, goals* and *key success factors.* The bulk of the chapter, however, focuses on *business processes* and the way that work activities are linked together to produce products and services for the customer.

MISSION AND GOALS

Your mission and goals spell out what your organization is being designed to do. They are important because, as the saying goes, "If you don't know where you're going, any road will get you there."

Mission

An organization's *mission* is the reason it exists. Every organization thus has a mission, even though it frequently is not spelled out in writing. A written *mission statement* is useful in communicating to the world your reason for existing, and also as a periodic reminder to employees of what you're all about.

A good mission statement:

◇ Describes your business purpose

◇ Reflects key customer needs and wants you are satisfying

◇ Creates the context for goal setting and planning.

Some examples of mission statements are given here.

Public Utility Company: *"To provide safe, reliable and economical energy services to customers at just and reasonable rates."*

Pharmaceutical Company: *"(Company) is an international biotechnology company that discovers, develops, manufactures and markets pharmaceuticals for significant medical needs."*

Rubbish Hauling Company: *"We haul anything that goes to the dump."*

Goals

Goals are results you intend to achieve. Your mission states what business you're in. Your goals state the concrete results you aim to get within a specified time period.

Goals commonly relate to:

◇ Financial results, such as profit margins, total sales, lower costs of production

◇ Customer concerns, such as quantity and quality of products and services, turnaround time for orders, cost of products.

To be useful, goals are:

◇ Measurable—it is clear whether or not they have been achieved

◇ Realistic—they can be reached in the time period stated and with the resources you have

◇ Challenging—they require you and your coworkers to put forward your best efforts.

As you develop your goals, it's a good idea at the same time to define how you're going to measure success on each one. Sometimes, this is obvious. For example:

Goal: *Sell 200 more widgets this year than last.*

How to measure: *Subtract number of widgets sold last year from number sold this year.*

Sometimes, it's not quite this easy.

Goal: *Increase customer satisfaction this year.*

How to measure: *Develop a customer satisfaction survey; administer it at the beginning of the year and again at the end. Compare the results.*

Chapter Five will present more information on ways to measure performance.

KEY SUCCESS FACTORS

Whereas a goal is a specific achievement you are aiming for within a specified time period, a key success factor is something you must pay attention to all the time. To identify key success factors for your business, ask yourself:

What must we do to be successful?

For a profit-making business, success means making a profit. Key success factors would vary depending on how that business makes its profit. For instance: for a business that produces low-cost clothing, key success factors might be having low-cost operations and high-volume sales. For a manufacturer of luxury women's clothing, costs wouldn't be as important as high quality—of material, construction and so on—and creative design.

In a future-oriented research and development company, high profit today may not be as critical as developing leading edge technology, producing innovative new products and building a good reputation that will attract investors.

As you evaluate alternative ways to design your organization, keep the key success factors in mind. Some design alternatives may clearly be better than others in helping you be successful.

BUSINESS PROCESSES

Being clear on mission, goals and key success factors are all preliminary to organization design. The first step in the design process itself is to identify the work that must be done to produce something of value for your customers and to see how this work is sequenced to form business processes.

What Is a Business Process?

A *business process* consists of the sequence of tasks and activities that must be completed to provide a product or service to the customer. To identify your business processes, you must ask yourself: What work needs to be done to produce our products and services, and how are the tasks and activities linked together? We'll use a simple domestic situation to illustrate.

Say that you want to give a dinner party. The process starts when it occurs to you that you would like to repay the hospitality of several friends. The end result of the process will be a dinner served to your friends.

The steps in the process are as follows.

1. You think, "I'd like to have a dinner party."

2. Prepare guest list, decide date and time, send out invitations.

3. Plan menu, select recipes.

4. Prepare grocery list, buy groceries.

5. Clean house.

6. Cook dinner, set table.

7. Guests arrive.

8. Serve dinner.

9. Guests express appreciation.

Obviously, this is a highly simplified version of the whole process. Some steps involve complicated subprocesses. Take "cook dinner," for example. You'll need to begin preparation of different dishes at different times; some can be prepared in advance, some will need to be cooking while other courses are being served. Each course has its own mix of ingredients, mustn't be over- or undercooked and must be coordinated with all the other courses so that everything is ready to be served at just the right time.

In terms of organization design:

◇ *First,* the end result or outcome—dinner on the table— corresponds to the product or service provided to customers.

◇ *Second,* the overall sequence of steps corresponds to a business process.

◇ *Third,* the more detailed set of tasks within each major step forms a subprocess.

Why Are Business Processes Important?

Probably everyone in an organization could easily name its major products and services. But many employees would be stumped if they were asked to describe their major business processes. This is because so often the work in a company is compartmentalized, and people in one department often have only a fuzzy idea of how other departments contribute to the same end product. Thinking through each business process can help each individual understand where and how their work fits into the overall picture.

Not only does this make work more meaningful to the average employee, but when everyone understands the ultimate point of what they are doing, it's easier for them to see how to make their part, as well as the overall product or service, more satisfying to the customer. It may also help employees see where a process can be made more efficient or even come up with new products and services.

Another reason it's important to understand your business processes is that this knowledge will guide you through the stages of organization design that follow. We'll return to this point later in the chapter.

Describing Business Processes

In thinking through the steps in a business process, it's helpful to think in terms of **end, start** and **in-between**. That is, start with the end result—the product or service that the process leads to. Next, note what step starts the process, and then identify each step in between. Consider the Enlok Windows example, which is diagrammed in Figure 1-1.

Enlok Windows manufactures and installs custom-designed windows in industrial buildings. One of its business processes involves "window replacement" in existing industrial buildings. (The process for providing windows for a new building is quite different.)

The *end result* is custom-designed windows that are installed at industrial sites to replace existing windows. The *starting point* is when the customer calls the sales office, explains the requirements, and asks for an estimate of cost. The *in-between* steps are items 2 through 9 on the figure.

Note that every step has its own outcome. For the salesperson, the sales order is an outcome; the estimator's final estimate is an outcome; the same is true of the engineer's drawings; the factory assembler's finished assembly; and so on. However, it is critical to the organization as a whole to understand that each of these interim outcomes is part of one process and that no one's work is truly done until the final product is installed at the customer's site to the customer's satisfaction.

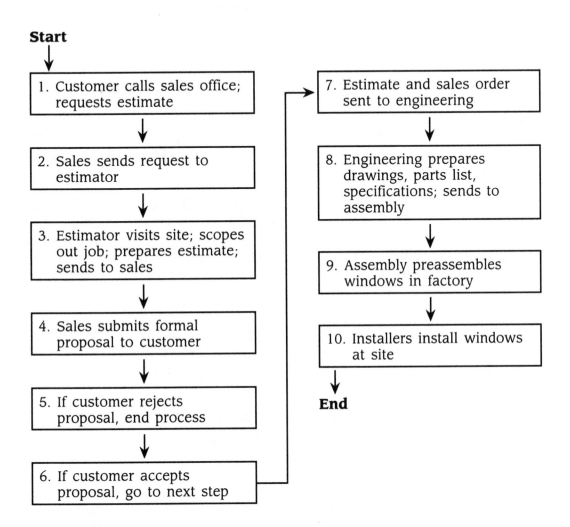

FIGURE 1-1. Enlok Windows business process: Filling customer order for replacement windows.

Start

1. Customer calls sales office; requests estimate

2. Sales sends request to estimator

3. Estimator visits site; scopes out job; prepares estimate; sends to sales

4. Sales submits formal proposal to customer

5. If customer rejects proposal, end process

6. If customer accepts proposal, go to next step

7. Estimate and sales order sent to engineering

8. Engineering prepares drawings, parts list, specifications; sends to assembly

9. Assembly preassembles windows in factory

10. Installers install windows at site

End

You can see how this process view of work departs from the view still prevailing in many organizations that can be summarized as: "My piece of work is done. I've thrown it over the wall to the next guy along the line, and it's now his responsibility."

As we mentioned earlier, this is only one business process for Enlok. Another key one for them is *filling orders for windows in new industrial buildings.* In the second process, because an order may tie up a lot of Enlok's resources, the company president may have to approve the decision to accept it. Also, in these cases, the customer's architect generally provides the specifications and drawings and new parts often have to be ordered from outside suppliers. It is a very different process from the first one.

Subprocesses

Earlier, we mentioned that each major step in a process will have one or more subprocesses associated with it. Take, for example, the subprocess that involves the estimator at Enlok. (This is diagrammed in Figure 1-2.)

The *end result* is that the estimate of time and cost is submitted to sales. The *starting point* is when the sales representative notifies the estimator of a customer's request. The *in-between* steps are those that occur between these two points. Subprocesses can be broken down for each task or position involved in a key process.

Workflow Charting

A very useful technique to use when you're trying to improve a process is workflow charting. This involves expanding each process and subprocess to show in detail every task and activity in that process. Work flowcharts often list not only the activity and sequence, but also who is involved at each step, length of time to complete each activity, the *inputs* (resources, information, and so on) fed into each step and the *outputs* of each step.

This level of detail can be extremely valuable in discovering how things are actually done and finding opportunities for improvement. For example, you might find that some tasks can be combined, or some steps eliminated altogether or work can be speeded up by changing the sequence of activities.

This level of detail is not usually necessary for the purpose of organization design. It is important, however, to understand the main business processes and major subprocesses, because this information will be helpful when you go through the design steps in the next chapters.

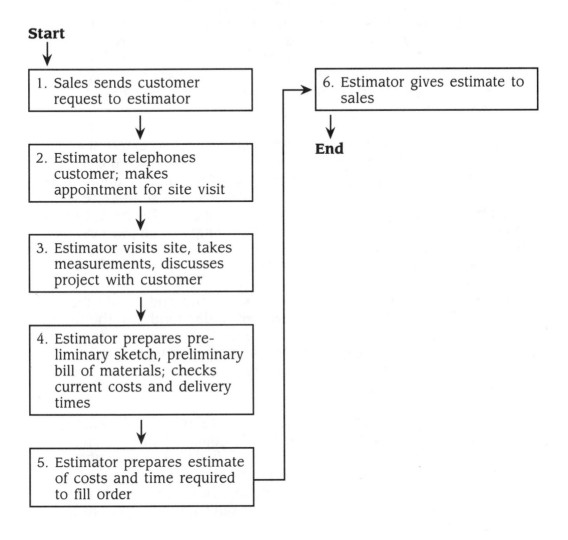

FIGURE 1-2. Enlok Windows subprocess: Preparing estimate for replacement windows.

Start

1. Sales sends customer request to estimator

2. Estimator telephones customer; makes appointment for site visit

3. Estimator visits site, takes measurements, discusses project with customer

4. Estimator prepares preliminary sketch, preliminary bill of materials; checks current costs and delivery times

5. Estimator prepares estimate of costs and time required to fill order

6. Estimator gives estimate to sales

End

Core and Noncore Processes

A *core* business process is one that is directly related to the organization's mission. *Noncore* processes may still be important but they aren't directly related to the mission.

Enlok Windows's mission is to design, assemble and install custom-made windows. The processes of filling customer orders, whether for new buildings or replacement windows, are thus core business processes. Enlok has a human resources depart-ment whose function is to make sure the company has a qualified workforce and to serve the needs of that workforce. This function is not directly related to the company's mission, and so the process through which human resources delivers its services is a noncore process.

Some companies make a deliberate decision to use external vendors for noncore work. Examples of work commonly contracted out include secretarial services, reprographics, artwork and building maintenance. Some companies even eliminate the need for a human resources department by hiring contract employees from employment agencies, which act as the employer: hiring and screening the employees, paying them, administering benefits, and so on. But most companies perform at least some noncore functions in-house.

Even though noncore work processes begin and end within the com-pany, it is critical that the people involved understand that the ultimate aim of internal processes is to support the company in serving customers. In some cases, staff programs appear to become ends in themselves, and their connection to customer service is lost. Consider the following example.

Some years ago, a major electric power company in the eastern United States instituted a companywide quality improvement program. Quality, the company claimed, boils down to doing a better job for the customers. The program was widely hailed in American business as a prime example of an excellent approach to quality, and the company won a prestigious industry award for quality.

Not long thereafter, however, trouble began. Workers com-plained that they spent more time on keeping quality records, attending quality meetings and showing visitors around their "prize-winning operation" than they did on the real work of serving customers. There was less recognition, they said, for making good business decisions than for following the quality-improvement process.

When a new executive officer took over in 1990, most of the program was dismantled, and the part that remains today is far less demanding of employees' time.

The message here is not that a quality program is always disruptive and interferes with service to the customer. Rather, it is that the underlying goal of any internal program is, or should be, to enable the company to serve customers better. If, in fact, the program gets in the way of serving customers, then the program must change.

Business Processes and Organization Design

Once you have spelled out your business processes, you will have essential information to use in designing your organization. For example, you will be able to see where steps in the work of your organization are interdependent and, therefore, where coordination and communication are especially important.

Interdependence is the extent to which two or more steps or tasks depend on each other. For example, the end result of one step is required for the next step to begin or to be completed. Or a mistake made in one step will lead to flawed results in the next step also.

Coordination is the linking together of different steps or tasks to produce the intended outcome.

To return to our dinner party example on page 12, groceries can't be purchased (4) until the menu is planned (3), nor can dinner be prepared (6) until the groceries have been purchased. These *interdependencies* mean that these activities must be sequenced in a certain way. On the other hand, cleaning house (5) could happen at any time.

If other people were helping you with the party arrangements, then *coordination* would become important. You would need to communicate with one another to make sure that nothing slips between the cracks and that you don't duplicate each other's work.

Remember the Enlok Windows example (Figure 1-1). Although all the steps are interdependent to some degree, some are much more so than others.

The second and third steps are not strongly interdependent. Sales gives a customer request to the estimator (#2), who then prepares the estimate (#3). The estimator does not depend on sales to get the information he needs for the estimate—rather, he contacts the customer himself, personally visits the site, and takes measurements.

If, instead, the estimator completely relied on information given to him by sales, there would indeed be high interdependence between these two steps. Sales' ability to submit a formal proposal to the customer (#4) is, of course, highly dependent on the results of the estimator's work.

As you can see, interdependence increases the need for coordination, which often depends on communication. Describing your business processes will illuminate where you need coordination, and this information will help you assess how good your organization design is.

It makes sense to have your business needs determine your structure rather than have your structure dictate how work is coordinated. In other words, "form should follow function." Ideally, activities that demand close coordination should be located near each other in the organization—if not physically, at least in the sense of being in the same organizational unit. Whether or not this is possible, the communication and coordination needs of interdependent activities should be designed into the organization, rather than left to chance.

Guidelines for Identifying Business Processes

Focus initially on your core business processes. The number of these will depend on the size of your organization and the number of products and services you provide. If the organization you're designing is a staff support unit within a larger organization, your business process or processes will likely be noncore. The important point is to see the connection between these noncore processes and the core business processes so that they all serve the ultimate goals of the whole organization. Each process will undoubtedly break down into a number of subprocesses, which you may find useful to examine in more detail.

Who Should Be Involved?

◊ ***Top level management.*** In small to midsized companies, the chief executive of the organization together with the executives who report to him or her would undoubtedly be able to name their major business processes and the steps within each. The larger an organization becomes, however, the more difficult it is for a limited number of even top people to be able to do this.

◊ ***Employees who represent each major step in the process.*** The more detail you're trying to capture, the more likely it is you'll want to involve the people who are closest to the work. They are most likely to understand the process that is *actually* followed in addition to the process that is *supposed* to be followed.

The first step is to identify your customers and the products and/or services you provide to each. Next, name the main process that results in each product or service (for example, *filling customer request for replacement windows*). Then for each process list every major step needed to accomplish the desired result.

An example of a worksheet format you might use follows. After going through the steps, it may be useful for you to diagram each business process and major subprocess. The simplest kind of diagram is the block flowchart, such as those that have been given in this chapter. Simply write out the steps, draw a box around each, and place them in sequence, with arrows to show the direction of flow. (See Harrington, 1991; Davenport, 1993; and Melan, 1992, for more on this subject.)

Worksheet

1. **Who are your customers—those people who use the products and services you provide? What product and/or service do you provide to each?**

   Customer   Product/Service

   _____

   _____

   _____

2. **Identify the major steps in the business process that results in each product or service.**

   First Business Process: _____

   (for example, *filling customer request for replacement windows*)

   Product/Service: _____
   (for example, *replacement windows*)

   First step: _____
   (for example, *customer calls sales with request*)

   Second step: _____

   Third step: _____

   And so on to last step

   Second Business Process: _____

   Product/Service: _____

   First step: _____

   Second step: _____

Third step: _____

And so on to last step

Repeat these steps for all business processes.

Next, list the steps for all necessary subprocesses (for example, *preparing estimates*).

3. Does it make sense to combine some of these processes? (For example, you may have two quite different products that are produced through the same process.) If so, which ones?

_____

_____

_____

4. If you haven't involved many other people in plotting out these processes, you may wish to get their input now on your findings.

First business process   People to involve/Their input

_____

_____

_____

_____

Second business process   People to involve/Their input

_____

_____

_____

_____

5. If your "organization" is a department that provides internal services only, add this additional question:

How do our noncore work processes contribute to the company's core business processes?

_____

_____

_____

You will be returning to this information on business processes when you come to make decisions on dividing up the work, forming a management structure and selecting coordination and control techniques.

Chapter Two

DIVIDING UP THE WORK

Once you have a good understanding of your mission and goals, the key success factors for your business and the core business processes through which you deliver products and services to customers, it is time to decide what kind of organization structure is best for you.

This chapter describes five types of organization structure:

1. Functional
2. Product- or Service-Based
3. Customer- or Geographical-Area Based
4. Business Process Teams
5. Matrix

Organization structure refers to the way work is divided up. To put it simply, structure is what the boxes and lines on the typical organization chart represent. The boxes show how work and respon-sibilities are clustered into units such as divisions, departments, sections and teams. The lines show the management structure—that is, who reports to whom or how the boxes relate to each other in the hierarchy. We discuss "boxes" in this chapter and "lines" in Chapter 3.

WHY STRUCTURE MATTERS

The larger the number of tasks to be done and the more people who are involved, the more important it is to split up work and workers into groups or units like divisions, departments and teams. There are different ways to do this, and the structure you end up with makes a big difference in terms of:

◇ What employees pay attention to

◇ The ease of coordinating activities

◇ The speed of producing goods

◇ The cost of running the business

◇ The nature and extent of supervision required

◇ Whom employees interact and build relationships with

In short, the structure of your organization can make all the difference to your ability to serve customers and stay in business.

DIFFERENT KINDS OF STRUCTURE

As we just mentioned, there are five basic ways to structure an organization—that is, around function performed, product or service, customers or geographical area served, business process and matrix. Many variations and combinations can be found. Large organizations are almost always *hybrids,* with one type of structure at the top level of the company and others at lower levels.

Each type of structure has relative strengths and drawbacks. Each one might be a good alternative in some situations and a poor alternative in others.

We will use the case of a hypothetical printing company, "ABC Printing," to illustrate the first four of the five structures.

ABC Printing produces letterhead, envelopes, brochures and business cards. It has a sales force, a staff of graphic designers and a print shop. It sells to large corporations, small businesses and individuals within the state and outside it and has a small international business.

1. Functional Structure

In a functional structure, units like divisions and departments are formed according to the major technical or professional function performed by the unit.

If ABC Printing had a functional structure, its departments would be Sales, Graphic Design and Print Shop. Each department would handle all products for both individual and corporate accounts, domestic and overseas.

FIGURE 2-1. Functional structure for ABC printing.

President

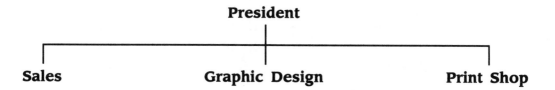

Sales   **Graphic Design**   **Print Shop**

Strengths of a functional structure are:

◇ It is easier to manage work *within* the group. This is because supervisors and subordinates share the same job-related knowledge.

ABC's graphic design manager was himself a graphic designer; thus, the schedules and standards he sets are realistic, and he can easily evaluate how well each designer is performing.

◇ Each group also contains people who "speak the same language" and who share and nurture each other's technical expertise. This kind of structure tends to attract and develop experts in each functional specialty. In businesses whose success depends on technical expertise, gathering and increasing that expertise can be an important competitive advantage.

In ABC's case, the designers will tend to gain a lot of technical expertise by interacting with one another. The more people there are in this department and the more varied their skills, the more this will be true. This concentration of talent could be critical to ABC's success.

◇ Labor costs are often lower than in any of the other alternatives we describe because people working on the same kind of task are in one "pool"—and workload can be more easily balanced as demand rises and falls for different products and different skills.

Drawbacks of a functional structure are:

◇ Often you need more than one department to complete a job. In these cases, coordination and communication between departments may be slower and less accurate than desirable. Misunderstandings may arise between departments that are responding to different pressures.

For example, ABC's salesperson may promise a customer a delivery date that the print shop can't meet.

◇ Because the involvement of all departments is needed to fill every customer order, each individual department manager has limited decision-making authority.

ABC's sales manager typically won't be able to authorize an unusual request from a customer without getting approval from the design and print shop managers.

◇ It may be difficult to develop new ways of doing business, especially if the new business requires unfamiliar cooperation across functional boundaries.

For example, at ABC Printing, new computer technology may enable the print shop to do graphic design. If organized functionally, these two departments may resist the indicated change and miss early opportunities to compete.

◇ Different departments will tend to have different priorities. Attempts to resolve conflicts between departments may be costly to the company in terms of time and money and may result in the customers' interests being overlooked.

Sales may be most concerned about speed of delivery, graphic design about quality of artwork regardless of the time involved, and the print shop about keeping costs low and having a steady flow of work.

◇ In this structure, it is often difficult to pinpoint accountability for results because each department can simply "pass the buck" to another.

If a customer complains about the product, sales may claim graphic design did not interpret the sales order correctly, design may claim that the print shop misunderstood the specifications, and the print shop may claim that it was given an unrealistic deadline.

◇ Finally, because this kind of structure tends to develop managers who specialize in a particular area, it is not as effective at developing all-round general managers who might be able to run the whole operation.

If ABC's general manager were to leave the company, it would be difficult to promote any one of the three functional managers to this position because their experience is in only one function. For example, the print shop manager does not have skills and experience in graphic design or sales.

2. Product- or Service-Based Structure

With this alternative, the organization forms departments or divisions around each of its products or services. Each department or division performs all the functions needed to produce its particular product or service.

So for ABC Printing, there would be a Stationery Division (letterhead and envelopes), a Brochures Division and a Business Cards Division. Each division has its own sales staff, graphic design staff and print shop for individual, corporate, domestic and overseas customers.

FIGURE 2-2. Product-based structure for ABC Printing.

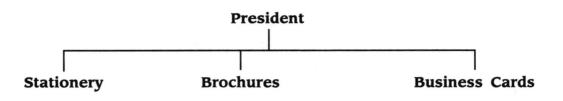

Strengths of a product- or service-based structure are:

◇ Responsibility for each product can be pinpointed at the division level.

If a customer is not satisfied with an order for brochures, the brochures division manager is responsible; he or she cannot blame another manager.

◇ Because everyone in a division focuses on just one product, that product is likely on the whole to be of higher quality, or more "state of the art," than products in a multiproduct division.

If ABC has a division that focuses on brochures only, it is more likely to become a "leading edge" brochure producer than if those employees spread their efforts among all the company's products.

◇ A team spirit will develop around each product line, and competition among divisions or departments can boost business all around.

At ABC, the stationery and brochures divisions may compete to get the most customers, the highest gross sales, or the highest profit margin, thus making the company as a whole more successful.

◇ A good candidate pool for top management can be developed, because each division manager will learn to manage several functions and will likely have more independence in making decisions.

For example, ABC's brochures manager will be adept at managing sales, graphic design and a print shop.

◇ Because division managers will have some independence in making decisions, they can respond more quickly to customer requests.

If a customer wanted an especially large format brochure, the ABC brochures manager could decide on his own whether or not to accept this order without having to wait for approval from the other managers.

Drawbacks of a product- or service-based structure are:

◇ There may be less sharing of resources across divisions and more duplication of effort, with resulting higher costs.

With this structure, ABC would end up with three groups of sales people, three groups of graphic designers and three print shops—one for each product line.

◇ Career opportunities may be restricted somewhat for professionals because their experience will be limited to just one product line.

For example, designers in the stationery division won't get experience in designing business cards or brochures.

◇ Customers who want multiple products and services will have to work with more than one division.

ABC's customers who want coordinated graphics in brochures, stationery and business cards will have to work with three different divisions.

◇ Because each division is an advocate for its own particular product, the company may be slow to recognize that a product should be changed, dropped or added.

The stationery division manager may urge the company to retain that product line even if it is no longer profitable.

3. Customer- or Geographical Area-Based Structure

In this alternative, the organization structures its major units around the characteristics or location of its customers or markets.

If ABC Printing were organized this way, it would have separate divisions to handle large corporate accounts, small businesses and individual accounts; or it might divide up geographically, with separate divisions to serve customers within the state, outside the state and overseas. Each division would handle all products and have its own sales, design and printing staff but would serve only one type of account or service area.

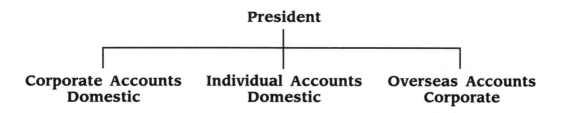

FIGURE 2-3. Customer-based structure for ABC Printing.

President

Corporate Accounts Domestic | Individual Accounts Domestic | Overseas Accounts Corporate

Strengths of a customer-based structure are:

◇ The unique needs of each type of customer are well served. The orientation of the company will be to meet customer needs.

For ABC, product and marketing requirements are likely to be quite different overseas as compared with the domestic market. There may be different language requirements and different cultural factors to consider. Corporate clients will require different credit arrangements and pricing than retail customers.

◇ The focus on customer or market keeps the company aware of changes in customers' needs and preferences, especially as compared to the product-based structure.

◇ Unprofitable product lines are more likely to be dropped than would be the case with either a functional- or product-based structure.

Drawbacks of a customer-based structure are:

◇ As with product-based structures, there may be less sharing of resources across division and department boundaries and more duplication of efforts and resulting higher costs.

◇ Internal systems may evolve in different ways to serve different customer segments. This may make overall management of the organization difficult.

For example, ABC might set up different accounting or inventory systems to handle its overseas customers and domestic customers, and this might make it difficult to compare results of the two market segments.

Dividing Up the Work

4. Business Process Team Structure

Teams have always been used by organizations to accomplish special, often temporary, projects. Today, they are a well-established way of getting work done and can be found in all types of organizations. Cross-functional teams are often given responsibility for complex assignments that fall outside the scope of the traditional departmental structure.

Teams are especially useful:

◇ When there is a need for flexibility and/or speed in handling projects such as special customer requests, product development or marketing campaigns.

◇ When it is important to have input from different parts of the organization simultaneously in completing a piece of work.

In Chapter 1, we discussed business processes and how important it is for everyone in an organization to understand the steps in each process. In recent years, some companies have begun to structure their organizations, or parts of them, around ongoing business process teams.

The business process team is characteristic of what is sometimes called a "horizontal organization," which has been in the limelight a great deal in recent years. (See, for example, Hammer and Champy, 1993, and Ostroff and Smith, 1992.)

A *horizontal organization* is one that structures work around its major work processes. It is called horizontal because the work units cut across traditional functions, rather than relying on a vertical hierarchy to coordinate activity. You will recall that a business process is the set of steps that results in a product or service for a customer. A business process team includes people who can perform all the major activities within a business process so that the members of a single team can collectively carry out the whole process from beginning to end.

In horizontal organizations, the focus is on whatever is involved in completing the work to satisfy customers. This kind of structure tends to reduce the number of levels of management. (It becomes a "flat" structure, as we describe in Chapter 3.)

> *Two core business processes for ABC Printing are filling orders for brochures for the domestic market and filling stationery orders for corporate accounts. If ABC were organized by business process, they would have a team (or teams) devoted to each of these processes. Each team would include people with skills in sales, graphic design and printing. The team would handle every step of the process from receipt of initial customer order to delivery of the completed order to the customer.*

Note that in each team shown in Figure 2–4, the sales, design and print shop members work as a team with their team leader handling only one kind of product for one customer type. Thus, their work is highly focused.

FIGURE 2-4. Business process team structure for ABC Printing.

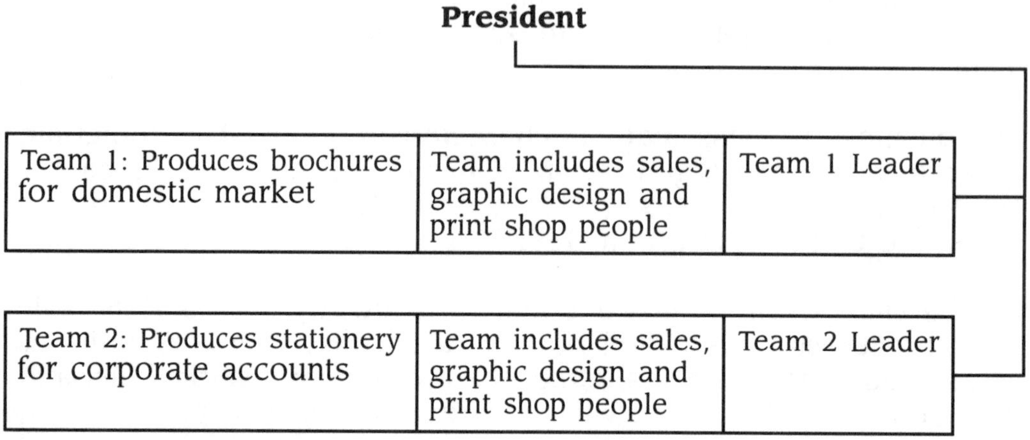

President

Team 1: Produces brochures for domestic market	Team includes sales, graphic design and print shop people	Team 1 Leader

Team 2: Produces stationery for corporate accounts	Team includes sales, graphic design and print shop people	Team 2 Leader

The teams report directly to the president. In a large company, it is likely there will be several brochures teams and several stationery teams, which may report to a brochures or stationery manager. Also, these teams have no technical support available within the company. In large companies, it's likely that there would be some design and printing experts to assist them.

Strengths of a business process team structure are:

◇ The focus of the organization is *outward to customers*, rather than *inward to a boss.*

◇ Time, and hence money, are saved because of the reduced need to pass information up and down the hierarchy and between departments.

For example, if a customer wants an order changed, the request would go to the team who would handle the request by itself. All the people who need to make decisions about the request are on the team.

◇ Business process teams promote self-management by employees and produce greater job satisfaction because of more worker involvement.

◇ People with different knowledge and skills work closely together on each team. This will broaden the knowledge and skills of each individual.

In ABC's business process teams, graphic designers will acquire new knowledge about sales and printing. The same is true of the people with a sales and printing background. This means that all people on this team will be able to talk with customers about all aspects of the work.

◇ There is speedier decision making, reduced cycle times and improved responsiveness to customers.

◇ Because it tends to "flatten" the organization—that is, reduce the number of levels of management—there are reduced management costs and less need for coordination.

Drawbacks of a business process team structure are:

◇ A successful redesign to a business process structure involves a major transformation of the organization. It is difficult, time consuming and probably very costly to make this change. New systems for virtually everything will be needed, from training, compensation and job appraisal to inventory, accounting and management information.

◇ This structure works best if each process team has within it sufficient expertise and team interaction skills to handle the issues that may arise; otherwise, the company must maintain functional experts to help out as needed.

For example, the graphic design members of ABC's teams must be skilled enough to handle all the design aspects of every customer request they get.

The horizontal structure may not be suited to every organization; however, the underlying philosophy is critical to every organization's survival today. This is the philosophy that *everyone involved in a work process* must understand the total process, how it serves customers and how he or she contributes to it!

Team members may have a single boss, the team leader. It is also possible, however, for members to serve on a process team and still be members of a regular functional department. In this case, each member would have two bosses: the team leader and the head of the functional department. This situation is called a *matrix*, and this is the fifth kind of structure we discuss.

5. Matrix Structure

A matrix structure occurs when an employee has two (or sometimes even more) bosses in the organization. It often accompanies the use of teams, such as project teams and business process teams. It is used when the organization wants both to gain the benefits of teams and maintain the technical expertise of functional departments.

> *One example is an engineering and construction company with departments representing the functional disciplines of civil, electrical and mechanical engineering. Teams are formed to carry out specific projects; each team typically has some civil, some electrical and some mechanical engineers reporting to a project leader. But all these engineers would also report to their functional managers: the chief civil engineer, chief electrical engineer or chief mechanical engineer.*

> *Over the course of a year, individual engineers might work for multiple project managers in addition to doing work directly for their chief engineer.*

Note that in Figure 2-5, the project manager has a mechanical, a civil and an electrical engineer reporting to him. Those engineers also report to the chief mechanical engineer, chief civil engineer and chief electrical engineer, respectively. The chiefs also have some engineers on their staffs who are not matrixed to the project manager. The contract engineer is not matrixed either; the project manager is his or her only boss. (At the end of the project, the contract engineer may be dismissed.)

Also, in this example, both the project manager and the engineering chiefs share authority over the matrixed engineers and have a major say in their promotions, raises and work.

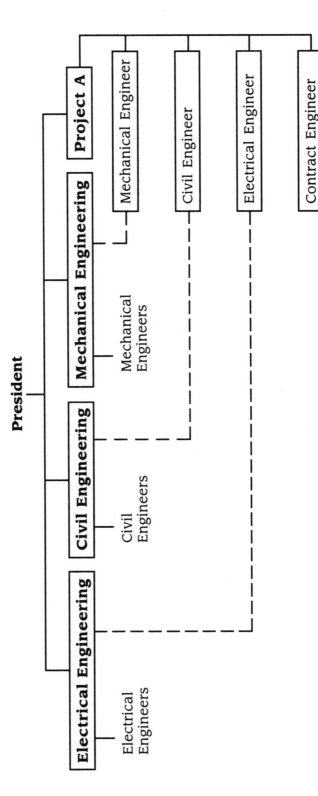

FIGURE 2-5. Matrix structure in an engineering company.

Strengths of a maxtrix structure are:

◇ It enables the organization to use its resources (people, money, facilities) efficiently. This is because resources are moved around as projects come and go. It provides the flexibility to assign staff according to project requirements and to reassign them quickly as project requirements change.

◇ This structure enables the organization to make full use of teams, and the advantages they possess, while maintaining in-depth technical expertise in critical functions.

◇ It gives individuals a chance to work with other employees with different skills and expertise, while still maintaining their own technical expertise (through their home department).

◇ It requires managers to cooperate with one another and moderates their power over their subordinates.

Drawbacks of a matrix structure are:

◇ In some cases, a matrix gets out of hand: Employees end up with multiple—not just two—bosses and the resulting confusion slows down decision making.

For example, until recently, Royal Dutch Shell had a matrix structure where some executives reported to a country, a regional and a functional head. These multiple relationships slowed down decision making and cost the company money. The company has now eliminated the matrix and established a more centralized operation.

◇ Having two or more bosses means an employee might have conflicting demands made on his or her time, and this can lead to personal stress and reduced work quality.

◇ Because resources are flexibly allocated in a matrix organization, and each manager's resources go up and down according to the work coming in, there are often power struggles between managers. These can disrupt the work and get in the way of good customer service.

◇ Subordinates might play one boss off against the other.

Engineer Bob Smith tells the project manager, "I'm sorry, I can't finish those calculations you needed today because my engineering chief needs me to work full-time on our department budget this week." But Bob Smith has omitted to say that his chief doesn't know he has promised work for the project manager—and could get someone else to work on the budget. Bob would rather work on the budget himself and so is manipulating the situation to make it seem there is no choice.

Making a Matrix Work

To make a matrix work for you, make sure each participant's role, responsibilities and authority are clearly defined, preferably in writing. At the same time, reward employees for being flexible and willing to "bend" for the good of the organization.

In the engineering company example, a certain mechanical engineer is assigned 75% time to a project manager and 25% time to the mechanical engineering department. However (and this is a common scenario), partway through, the project runs into unexpected difficulties and this engineer is needed full-time to help out. If the chief agrees to this reassignment, the department's work will fall behind. But the chief's work is not as high priority as the project, so the reassignment of this engineer is to the benefit of the company.

Be especially clear about performance evaluations for the matrixed employees. People naturally tend to pay more attention to the person who will be evaluating them and determining promotions and raises. Make sure that everyone for whom an employee produces work (and this could include customers) gives input to that employee's performance evaluation.

6. Hybrid Organizations—Mixing and Matching Structures

When all is said and done, most larger organizations—and a lot of smaller ones too—are hybrids. That is, within each of them there is a mixture of structural forms.

For example, take a giant corporation like General Motors. Figure 2-6 shows a small segment of General Motors's corporate organization chart, as it was structured in 1993.

FIGURE 2-6. Portion of General Motors corporate organization chart.

CEO & President

```
North American
Truck Platforms

North American
Passenger Car Platforms

North American
Vehicle Sales, Service
& Marketing

Automotive Components Group
Worldwide

GM Powertrain Group
```

```
                                    Executive VP

                                    General Motors
                                    Europe
```

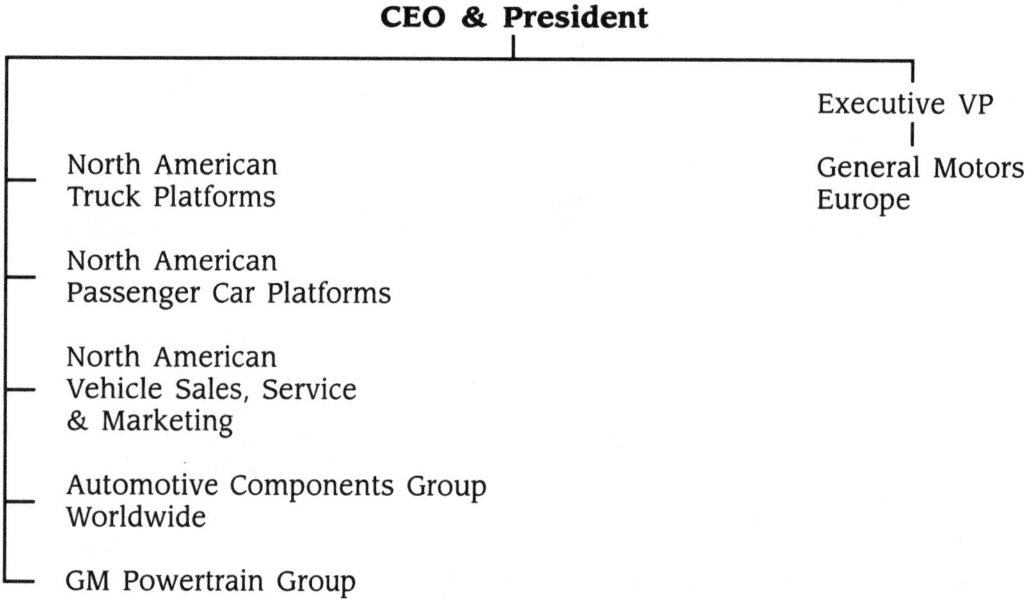

This structure is partly *product-based* (truck platform, passenger car platform, and so on) and partly *customer- or market-based* (North America, Europe). Figure 2-7 shows the next organizational level down for one of these groups, North American Vehicle Sales, Service & Marketing.

This shows that some divisions are based on *product* (for example, Buick and/or Oldsmobile) and some on *function* (for example, marketing and/or sales policy).

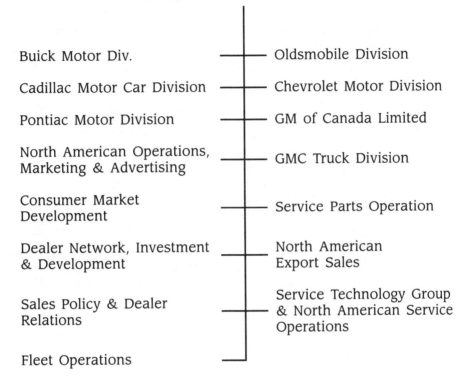

FIGURE 2-7. Portion of General Motors corporate organization chart.

**North American Vehicle
Sales, Service & Marketing**

Buick Motor Div. —————— Oldsmobile Division

Cadillac Motor Car Division ———— Chevrolet Motor Division

Pontiac Motor Division ———— GM of Canada Limited

North American Operations, ———— GMC Truck Division
Marketing & Advertising

Consumer Market ———— Service Parts Operation
Development

Dealer Network, Investment ———— North American
& Development   Export Sales

Sales Policy & Dealer ———— Service Technology Group
Relations   & North American Service
                                              Operations

Fleet Operations ————

Points to Ponder

Think of two or three organizations that you know fairly well and how each one is structured.

1. If they have hybrid structures, what are they, and why do you think they were chosen?

2. What might be the consequences of choosing a different way of structuring (for example, blending functional departments into product-based departments)?

Dividing Up the Work

GUIDELINES FOR CREATING AN ORGANIZATION STRUCTURE

Who Should Be Involved?

The first question to answer is, "Who should be involved?" The extent to which employees are involved in creating a structure varies. Sometimes the boss works it all out alone or every employee in the organization might participate. And there might be any degree of involvement in between these two extremes. Some points to consider in deciding what makes sense in your situation are these.

◇ The more involvement people have in creating something, the more committed they will be to making it work.

◇ For their ideas to make sense and help the organization thrive, the involved employees must be both knowledgeable about the organization's business situation and committed to its success.

◇ Involvement takes time. If a decision to change the organization has to be made in a hurry, you may have to choose a less democratic process. (You don't seek consensus before moving people out of a burning building!)

Whoever is involved, it is essential that each person understands his or her role in the design project. For instance, are participants expected to:

• Give input only?

• Make recommendations to management?

• Comment on management proposals?

• Actually make design decisions?

Make sure that all boundaries and limitations are made clear at the start. For example, sometimes management knows at the outset that they will not approve any new design that increases costs or increases work force size. It is essential the design team members know this before they start proposing design alternatives.

Whether the design is the primary responsibility of the manager in charge or that of an employee design team, the basic questions to ask and steps to take are the same.

Case Study:
Trist Technology Redesign Process

Trist Technology (TT) is a company whose founder, Talbot Trist, helped originate local area network (LAN) hardware and software. These technologies allow computers inside a building or between nearby buildings to share resources and communicate with one another. Like many other Silicon Valley companies, TT is technology-driven in that the founder developed a promising technology and built the company around it. The company thus ended up being designed around its research and development (R&D) function, with the technology perfected into products that are then marketed to customers.

With growing competition, TT has lost market share and money. Although its R&D department has always designed state-of-the-art hardware and software, it has been far less adept at customizing the technology to meet customer needs. The current CEO and the senior managers decided they needed to reexamine their current organization and see if a change in structure was warranted.

This is a very concise summary of their responses to the questions we pose and steps we suggest taking. (see pp. 52–56)

Questions to Ask

1. How is your organization structured now?

The current organization has a functional structure, as shown here.

FIGURE 2-8. Trist Technology current structure.

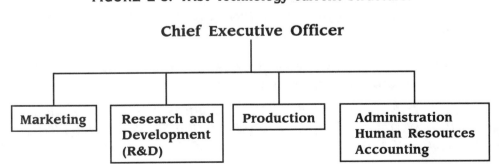

2. What are the strengths and drawbacks of this structure?

Strengths:

- *Fosters strong technical expertise. Our products are leaders in the industry.*

- *Morale is high, especially among R&D employees who believe their work is "cutting edge."*

Drawbacks:

- *R&D tends to work in a vacuum, being too technology-driven and getting increasingly out of touch with what customers really want and what their problems are in using our products.*

- *Although marketing representatives are engineers, they do not communicate enough with R&D people to anticipate and help resolve technical problems customers have with our products.*

- *This kind of structure doesn't promote the close working relationships between marketing and R&D that would improve this situation.*

3. How does your current structure serve or fail to serve the needs of your customers?

- *They express frustration that we seem more intent on developing fancy technology than in understanding what their needs are and developing products to fill their needs.*

- *They'd like to have direct access to technical people who can understand their problems and propose solutions.*

- *They really like the informal teams we use at times where a group of technical and marketing people get together to solve a problem for a customer. Customers say we need more of these teams.*

4. How are your business processes helped or hindered by your current structure?

We have two somewhat different business processes through which we deliver hardware products and software, but there are similar problems with the way each one works.

- *Each business process is too R&D-driven. R&D not only develops the prototypes of new products, but often "follows" them into production—sometimes continuing to tweak hardware and even rewrite software code as products are readied for delivery to customers.*

- *Marketing representatives are essentially left out of the loop. It's difficult for them and for customers to know how TT can meet customers' needs.*

- *Once hardware and software are delivered to customers, it's hard for them to get technical support in using the technology.*

5. How do your employees feel about the current structure?

- *Employees on the whole are comfortable with our present structure and are worried about how change may affect them.*

- *On the other hand, increasing numbers of employees, especially those in R&D, are frustrated that customers so often have difficulty using our products. These employees say they would like to have the time and opportunity to work directly with customers as part of their regular job.*

- *All employees understand that the company is getting out of touch with the users of its products and that this is causing it to lose business. They understand that some change is necessary.*

6. How might a different structure eliminate or improve weaknesses in the current one?

- *Business process teams would help to pull together R&D, sales and manufacturing; but it would be time consuming and costly to redesign the whole organization around teams. Also, breaking up the high-performing R&D department would really weaken the company's ability to develop new state-of-the-art hardware and software fast enough to stay ahead of the competition.*

- *A customer- or market-focused structure presumably would focus our efforts on our customers. The problem is we don't have very clear market segments that we could split up into. The main distinction we could make is between large corporate customers and small businesses, and it's not clear how splitting into two divisions for "large" and "small" customers would really resolve the issues.*

- *We could reorganize according to product: hardware or software. This would, if anything, increase the high technical quality of R&D. If hardware and software were designed to work with competitors' software and hardware respectively, it would greatly expand TT's potential market. The manager in charge of each division would be held responsible for customer satisfaction and thus would be motivated to see that customer needs are met.*

Steps in the Design Process

A. Decide what's most important to you, in order of importance.

1. *Increasing market share and profitability.*

2. *Maintaining our technical superiority in LAN hardware and software.*

3. *Becoming responsive to the users of our products—helping them use what we develop and understanding their needs so we can customize products to meet those needs.*

4. Minimizing costs to stay competitive.

B. Draw up several alternative structures.

The only alternative that we'd like to explore is the product-focused structure. If we were to reorganize strictly according to this, the chart would look like Figure 2-9.

C. Evaluate each alternative in terms of advantages and drawbacks.

Likely advantages of this product-based structure.

- *Forming product-focused divisions means that the company will likely maintain, and probably increase, its technical excellence.*

- *Each division manager, especially if the divisions are profit centers, will be strongly motivated to increase profits and market share.*

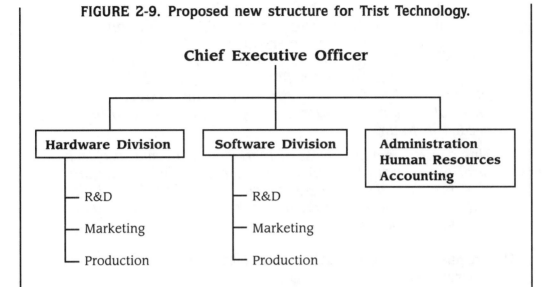

FIGURE 2-9. Proposed new structure for Trist Technology.

Chief Executive Officer

| Hardware Division | Software Division | Administration Human Resources Accounting |

Hardware Division
— R&D
— Marketing
— Production

Software Division
— R&D
— Marketing
— Production

- *Each division will be free to pursue other markets for its outputs; that is, the hardware division can design hardware to work with other vendors' software; the software division can make their software work with other vendors' hardware. This would increase the company's overall sales and further stimulate competitive technical excellence in each division.*

- *Each division manager will be accountable for pulling together the work of marketing, R&D and manufacturing to do whatever is needed to serve customers better, and thus enhance sales.*

- *Each division manager will be motivated to run an efficient operation, thus keeping costs low and increasing profits.*

Possible drawbacks of this product-based structure:

- *This calls for marketing to be split up between the two product divisions. Typically, a customer has both hardware and software needs and this change would mean the customer will have to work with two marketing representatives, not one as at present.*

- *This new structure doesn't directly address the issue of needing R&D people to have direct access to customers.*

One solution is to vary this structure by creating a third division, Integration Services. This would have the mission of working directly with customers to understand their needs, find solutions to their technical problems, help them adapt the company's hardware and software offerings to their own situation, and feed back information to the product divisions on what sorts of hardware and software are likely to be needed in future.

This division would consist of marketing staff and also technical people from the R&D departments. By its very nature, it is a "bridging" division between customers and the technical divisions. We have thus created a "service" division to add to the two product divisions.

D. Prepare an organization chart to show your preferred alternative(s).

Below is a chart of the amended organization.

FIGURE 2-10. New structure for Trist Technology (final version).

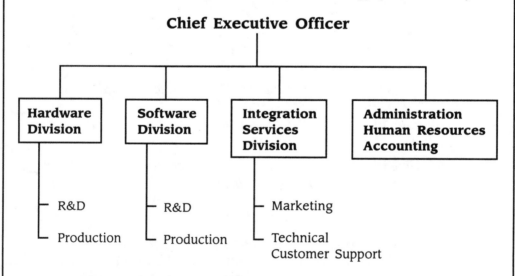

E. Get feedback from others.

- *Customers like the new structure because it gives them access to the technical people they need to help them use their LAN hardware and software effectively.*

- *Those R&D people remaining in the hardware and software divisions are satisfied because they are free to continue developing innovative technology.*

- *Those R&D people who most enjoy working with customers and solving practical application problems will likely be transferred to the new Integration Services division. They anticipate this will greatly increase their personal job satisfaction in addition to helping the customers.*

- *All employees are somewhat apprehensive, although most employees feel it is worth trying out the new structure, given its apparent advantages. In particular, the new organization calls for strong collaboration between the Integration Services division on the one hand and the two product divisions on the other. Also, the idea of the hardware and software divisions' having to compete against outside suppliers makes some employees uncomfortable.*

The following is a worksheet format that repeats the same questions posed to Trist Technology.

Worksheet

Start by answering the questions below. Your answers will help point out what's working well and what can be improved with your current structure. We have used a case study (see pages 45–51) to show how one high technology company, Trist Technology, answered the same questions as it went through a recent organization redesign process.

Questions to Ask

1. How is your organization structured now? (Draw a chart.)

2. What are the strengths and drawbacks of this structure? (It might be useful to ask others inside and outside the organization.)

_____

_____

_____

3. How does your current structure serve or fail to serve the needs of your customers? (Ask them.)

_____

_____

_____

4. **How are your business processes helped or hindered by your current structure?** (Think about coordination needs—for example, which steps in each business process are highly interdependent?)

_____

_____

_____

5. **How do your employees feel about the current structure?** (Ask them if a different structure might improve their morale, productivity, opportunities for creativity?)

_____

_____

_____

6. **How might a different structure eliminate or improve weak-nesses in the current one?**

_____

_____

_____

Steps in the Design Process

The following are steps to take whether you're designing a brand new organization or trying to improve an existing one. On pages 45–51, we show the summarized responses of the design team at Trist Technology as they went through these steps.

A. **Decide what's most important to you, in order of importance.** (Think back to key success factors, goals, and business processes discussed in Chapter 1. Which of these might be affected by your structure?)

_____

_____

_____

B. Draw up several alternative structures. (On paper, draw up two or more alternative ways to structure your organization. It helps to have employee participation at this point. It's okay to be playful at first, and essential to keep an open mind.)

C. Evaluate each alternative in terms of advantages and drawbacks. Judge each alternative structure according to the prioritized factors you decided on in step A above. One alternative may clearly be the winner. Or you may wish to combine features of more than one alternative to get a structure that is right for you. Narrow the alternatives down to no more than two or three.

_____

_____

_____

D. Prepare an organization chart to show your preferred alternative(s). (On paper, draw your preferred alternatives. In addition, it's a good idea to list out the main functions and responsibilities for each of the "boxes.")

E. Get feedback from others. You will need feedback from those who will have to make the new structure work (managers, employees) and others who will or may be affected by it, for example, labor unions, customers, suppliers.

Asking for Feedback on Proposed New Structure

Whether or not you involve others in creating a new organization structure, it is very important that you get their ideas on what you propose to do *before you try to implement it.*

Prepare an organization chart that lists out the major functions of each department shown. Get input from the people who have to make it work and the people who will be affected by it in a major way. Consider:

Customers   Suppliers

Employees   Community groups

Other departments (if part   Regulators (if a regulated
of a larger company)   company)

Labor unions

Ask questions like the following:

◇ What do you like about this proposed organization structure?

◇ What things do you think would work better if we changed to this?

◇ What things do you not like about it? Why not?

◇ What changes can you suggest that would make it work better?

◇ What would we need to do to make sure this gets implemented smoothly?

More specifically, what would be the likely impact of these suggested changes on:

• Getting important work done?
• Coordinating tasks in a business process?
• Staffing levels?
• Rewards and benefits?
• Need for training?
• Bargaining unit agreements?
• Work space, facilities and equipment?
• Information systems?
• Communications—inside and outside the company?
• Costs of production?
• Community relations?
• Any other important factors in your organization?

F. Revise and finalize the structure. Review the information you get from step E. This will help you choose one alternative if you had more than one resulting from step C. It will also undoubtedly lead to some fine-tuning of the final choice.

If you would really like to try something new, but are not sure it will work:

◇ If it's a *small change,* do it anyway. Keep an eye on it, and be prepared to modify or reverse your decision if things don't work out.

◇ If it's a *big change*, consider having a pilot test. Set up the pilot for a specified time period, and have "before" and "after" measures of the factors that are critical to your organization's success. Be fully prepared to make major adjustments to your proposed new structure if things don't work out. Do not prepare people to make the pilot succeed at any price!

You have just completed one important part of designing an organization—deciding how to divide up the work. It is now time to consider the next major piece of organization design—the management structure.

Chapter Three

MANAGEMENT STRUCTURE

Management structure consists of three main factors: the *hierarchy* or number of management levels, the *span of control* and how *centralized* or *decentralized* decision making in the organization is. First, some definitions.

Management hierarchy refers to the number of levels of management and supervision. A *flat* structure is one with few levels; a *tall* structure has many levels.

Span of control refers to the number of people who report to one manager or supervisor. If there are very few people, we call this a *narrow* span of control; if there are many people, we call it a *broad* span of control.

An organization is *centralized* to the extent that major decisions, control over resources and authority to take action are in the hands of only a few top people; it is *decentralized* to the extent people at lower levels are able to make decisions, control resources and take action in their part of the organization.

These factors are closely linked. For instance, any time a company adds a level of management, assuming it does not add to its total number of employees, its average span of control will become narrower. Figure 3-1 illustrates how span of control changes when an

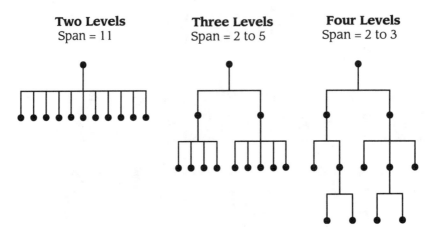

FIGURE 3-1. Spans of control and levels of management.
(Total number of people in each example = 12)

Two Levels
Span = 11

Three Levels
Span = 2 to 5

Four Levels
Span = 2 to 3

organization moves from two to three to four levels. Of course, the reverse is also true.

MANAGEMENT HIERARCHY

All people who draw a paycheck from an organization are *employees.* *Managers* are those people who are responsible for directing, coordinating and controlling the work of others. It is common to refer to the people who report to a manager as *subordinates;* however, this term may have a connotation of inferiority, and throughout this book we generally use the word *workers,* rather than subordinates, to refer to nonmanagerial employees.

There are three levels of management. Top-level managers are those occupying the highest positions in the organization. A small company may have only one top-level manager: the proprietor or president. The larger the company, the more top-level managers there will be; they will generally be the people who report directly to the Chief Executive Officer (CEO).

First-level managers are those who directly supervise workers. In a big organization, this is the lowest level of management. Middle-level managers are those occupying management levels in between the top level and the first level. Large companies often have several levels of middle management. Today, increasing numbers of business firms are reexamining the need for some of their middle-management positions, and these positions are prime targets for elimination in efforts to "flatten" the organization (as we describe later).

All these levels form what is called a *hierarchy* or *chain of command.* Power, authority and influence typically—although not always, as we shall see—increase the higher a person is in this hierarchy.

Power in an organization is defined as the ability to control the actions and decisions of others even if they resist. A person who holds a high position in an organization has power by virtue of that position; this is called *positional power.*

Authority refers to the right to make decisions—about what others should do and how they do it, how much money to spend on what, and so on. Authority is formally granted by the organization; it is thus *legitimate power.*

Influence is the ability to affect what others do or believe, regardless of whether or not one has the authority to do so.

Accountability refers to the state of being held answerable for results.

Exceptions to the Rule

We said earlier that there are exceptions to the general rule that the higher up the hierarchy a person is, the greater that person's power, influence and authority. Exceptions occur:

◇ When people at lower levels have special knowledge, skills or external connections not shared by those at higher levels and these are critical to that organization's success.

One example: *Technical experts in nonmanagerial positions in high technology companies often exert considerable influence on the company's decisions; sometimes their salaries are greater than employees at higher levels.*

Another example: *A company's political lobbyist who forms powerful connections with lawmakers in Washington or the state capital may have more influence in the company, due to these outside connections, than many people at higher levels.*

◇ When the company has bargaining-unit contracts.

   In the past, labor unions have exerted considerable power over organizations and much influence over their employee members. Consider how much power union workers hold over management when they threaten to strike.

◇ When a lower-level person is in a position that allows him or her to control access to higher-level positions.

   Frequently, a high-level executive's secretary has the power, though not the authority, to control who gets to see the executive. This person may have influence too if the boss has confidence in her or his judgment.

◇ When authority is delegated to lower levels. In some cases, people who have the authority to make certain kinds of decisions may delegate that authority to people at lower levels. Typically, in these cases, both the person delegating and the person delegated to will share accountability for results.

   For example, a department manager may have the authority to hire and fire all employees in that department. He may delegate this authority to the first-level supervisors who report to him, because he feels they are better able to judge the qualifications and performance of their workers. With formal delegation of this authority, the first-line supervisors do not have to get the manager's approval any time they hire or fire someone. But both manager and supervisors are jointly accountable for the overall level and quality of staffing in the department.

Flat and Tall Hierarchies

It obviously makes a big difference to the individual where in the hierarchy he or she is placed. It also makes a big difference to the organization how many management levels it has. Every management level added to or removed from the organization affects how work is done, the way employees feel about their work and the cost of management.

Adding a Level

An example will help to illustrate what typically happens when a company adds an extra level of management.

When Bill Beaumont started his machine shop, Beaumont Machining, he had three employees: one to handle the office work and two machinists. Then his business expanded, and he hired two more machinists. With more of his time spent in managing the overall business, he had less time for resolving the day-to-day issues that arose in the machine shop. So Bill appointed his senior machinist, Manuel, to be supervisor over the other three machinists.

Thus Beaumont Machining moved from a two-level organization to a three-level one, at least in the machine shop (see Figure 3-2). Note that this is still a two-level organization as far as the office administrator position is concerned.

FIGURE 3-2. Beaumont Machining.

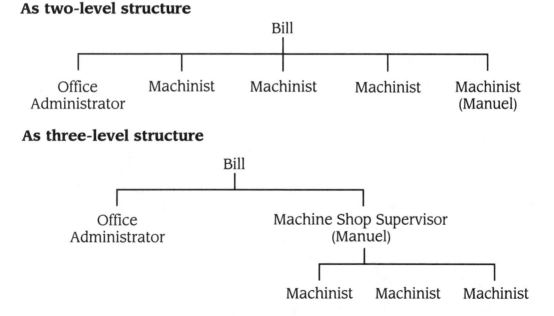

As two-level structure

As three-level structure

Consider what impact this additional level of organization has on Bill, Manuel and the three machinists.

◇ *Bill is now freed from having to manage the day-to-day issues that arise in running the machines; he thus has a lot more time available to spend on getting new business, working with customers and managing company finances.*

◇ *Manuel now has a chance to learn some supervisory skills and make many more decisions than he did previously. As he becomes adept at handling personnel issues, work scheduling and quality control, he will even further relieve the load on Bill.*

◇ *The three machinists find Manuel much more available to answer questions and help resolve problems than Bill was, given Bill's much broader range of responsibilities. On the other hand, they are now one step removed from the "boss." Suggestions and concerns they have must first be referred to Manuel who may then need to consult Bill.*

◇ *Manuel, in his position as go-between, has the opportunity to slow down or speed up, clarify or distort communication between Bill and the machinists, and vice versa. Manuel can ease Bill's load by reducing the amount of information that Bill receives; however, problems may arise if Bill gets too far out of touch with issues in the machine shop.*

Removing a Level

Here's an example of what happens when a company removes a level of management.

Personnel Services International (PSI) provides human resources services to corporations throughout Europe and North America. Until recently, it had a head office in the United States, 17 regional offices (14 in North America and three in Europe, and local offices in all major metropolitan areas on both continents.

While its business has been growing steadily, its profit margins have been getting smaller and its competition fiercer. After a major corporate review of cost-cutting opportunities, PSI decided to eliminate its regional offices. Some employees have been reassigned to local offices or to corporate headquarters, but many have been discharged.

Thus, PSI moved from a three-level company to a two-level one. Consider the impact of the removal of the regional level on the local offices as well as on employees at corporate headquarters.

◇ *Managers of the local offices and their employees have more autonomy and responsibility—to generate and fulfill new business contracts, to keep track of financial and accounting information, to staff and manage projects and to ensure customer satisfaction in all areas.*

◇ *The support that people in the local offices used to get from the regional staff is no longer available; some support is available from headquarters, but there are fewer people there so it often takes longer to get help.*

◇ *The systems developers at corporate headquarters interact more with the local offices; this means they get a lot of information useful to development efforts about what works and what doesn't in different situations. Before, this information was routed through the regional offices and much of what was eventually passed on to headquarters was inaccurate or incomplete.*

◇ *Corporate finance and accounting staff have to manage and reconcile all the information coming in from local offices. There are no regional staff to help them with this, nor to blame for problems.*

We have used one small company and one fairly large company as examples, but note that the effects are similar no matter how large or small the organization. In fact, we can make the following statements about flat and tall organization structures.

In a flat organization—that is, one with relatively few management levels—

◇ Communication throughout the organization is generally faster and less distorted.

◇ Decisions can be made faster, which means that the company can be quicker in responding to customers.

◇ Employees at lower levels feel more in touch with top management.

◇ The support that could be provided by more levels of management must be obtained by other means: by having more self-sufficient employees at the lower levels or in the way work is done.

◇ On the downside, there are fewer opportunities for promotion as there are fewer levels to move up to.

In a tall organization—that is, one with relatively numerous levels—

◇ Because the average span of control is narrower, the supervisory load is less for each manager. Tighter supervision may in some cases result in more productive work units—for example, when low productivity and poor quality of results appear to result from workers' not understanding or not following procedures. See the "Mail Room" case study for an example of this.

◇ There are more opportunities for promotion because there are more "steps in the ladder" for people to climb.

◇ Communication is slower and likely to be less accurate. This is because:

1. *The more links there are in a communication chain, the greater the likelihood of distortion.*

We are all familiar with the parlor game where one person in the room whispers a sentence to the next person, who whispers it to the next person, and so on. The version the last person hears is usually a far cry from the original.

2. *People tend to communicate more easily with others at the same organizational level.*

Information tends to get filtered as it moves up or down a level. Upper-level managers sometimes withhold facts from workers (saying "they don't need to know") but these facts may be very important for workers to know.

Additionally, workers are often reluctant to pass on bad news to higher levels.

◇ Decisions take longer to make. This is especially true where there is a tall functional management structure that requires coordination across the functional boundaries. See the "American Auto Industry" case study for an example of this.

Case Study:
Adding an Extra Level in the Mail Room

The poor performance of the mail room in a large West Coast firm was a company joke. Mail took longer to get from the company mail room to the addressees within the firm than it did to arrive at the company from overseas. It was constantly misdirected, and frequently important documents were lost, often greatly disrupting company business.

One supervisor directed the work of 20 mail clerks. Although sorting procedures were adequate, the clerks frequently didn't understand them or take the trouble to follow them. Discipline was poor and many people took overly long breaks and engaged in much nonwork-related gossip. Whenever major problems arose, there was much finger pointing and shirking of responsibility.

An industrial engineer called in to recommend solutions to this unfortunate situation suggested that an additional supervisory level be created: consisting of three first-line supervisors to report to the existing manager. (This manager, of course, then moved from being a first-line to a middle manager.) The three new supervisors were promoted from the existing pool of clerks; no additional clerks were hired so the total headcount of the department remained the same.

In spite of the fact that salary costs rose somewhat (the supervisors received an increase in pay), the company immediately reaped benefits from this extra management level. With closer supervision of the clerks: (a) established procedures were followed, (b) the clerks' questions were answered quickly (the former

---

single manager just didn't have the time to help everyone), c) because employees were formed into teams under each supervisor, a somewhat competitive team spirit arose, leading to higher morale, less malingering and higher productivity.

All this resulted in the mail being delivered faster and with fewer mistakes.

Case Study:
Chimneys in the American Auto Industry

American automobile manufacturers are known for their historic difficulties in coordinating work across functional boundaries. Some writers have described these multileveled functional departments as *chimneys* or *silos*. Different departments that need above all to work effectively together for the good of the company have instead tended to perceive one another as villains.

Engineering and Design were often accused by Manufacturing of designing vehicles that could not be built, with specifications that could not be met. Quality Assurance was viewed as the enemy of Production because inspectors could tag any vehicle anywhere in the assembly line for diversion to a repair bay. It could ruin a day's production numbers when many vehicles ended up in repair.

With the negative emotions aroused, it is easy to see how difficult it was for managers of these different functions even to communicate, much less coordinate their work.

Problems of this kind were so serious at Ford in the late 1970s and early 1980s the company's survival was at stake. In building the Taurus and Mercury Sable models, Ford dramatically changed the way these and subsequent cars were built. Now, cross-functional teams work closely together to design and test each new model. These teams represent all the different stages of the product-development process: designers, marketers, engineers, manufacturers, suppliers and factory-floor workers.

Organization Size and Structure

Size is one of the most important variables affecting an organization's structure. As they grow, most organizations follow a similar evolutionary pattern, as illustrated in Table 3-1.

When an organization starts out as a one-person enterprise (stage 1 in the table), that person performs all the tasks he or she is capable of doing, and contracts out the rest to external providers. For example, if this is a manufacturing business, the owner/proprietor may handle sales, design and manufacture of the product, delivery and billing. He or she may contract out secretarial and bookkeeping services, janitorial and legal services.

As the company grows (stage 2), the owner will hire some employees, and these people will likely specialize in certain functions. So a division of labor appears. For example, the owner may hire a sales representative, a product designer and a machinist to make the product. The owner may also hire an office administrator to handle

	Company Size	No. of Levels	Division of Work
TABLE 3-1. Evolution of a hypothetical organization as size increases.			
Stage 1: Single owner	1	1	None—one person does it all
Stage 2: Hires four employees	5	2	Individuals perform specialized functions
Stage 3: Departments formed. First-level supervisors hired	50	3	Functional departments
Stage 4: Middle management level created	500	4	Functional departments
Stage 5: Multiple levels of middle management	5,000	4–8	Functional or product/customer focused
Stage 6: Functional organization becomes unwieldy	50,000	6–12	Product/customer focused divisions
Stage 7: Company tries to recapture benefits of "smallness"	65,000	"Flattens" 4–6	Divisions as profit centers and autonomous operations

secretarial and bookkeeping work and so will reduce the amount of work contracted out.

At stage 3, as the company gets even bigger, we will find departments rather than individuals to handle functions so another level of management is added: a sales manager to handle a group of sales representatives, a design manager to manage a group of designers, and so on.

As the organization gets bigger still (stage 4), middle levels of management appear. Now the sales department may be split up into several sections according to the territory served: each section will have a first-line supervisor managing it, first line supervisors will report to the sales manager, who reports to the president.

Initially, most organizations start by being functionally organized. When they become large (stage 5), they often split into divisions that are organized by product, customer or geographical area served. These divisions often have functional departments within each. (Refer back to the General Motors organization charts in Chapter 2.)

By the time an organization grows extremely large (stage 6), it is common to find that it spends more time and resources on maintaining itself than on serving its customers. Today, when being attentive to and responding quickly to changing markets is critical to survival, these top-heavy companies find that their size inhibits their ability to compete successfully.

A large organization is very slow to change, even when its managers understand the need to do so. It has been compared to an ocean liner that simply cannot stop in its tracks or change course in an instant even if its captain is alert enough to spot danger ahead.

Large companies try in different ways to capture the speed and flexibility of smaller companies (stage 7). Sometimes, they split into comparatively independent divisions—becoming, in effect, a cluster of "little companies."

> For example, some years ago, Hewlett-Packard Corporation found that its growing size was hindering its ability to succeed in the highly competitive scientific instrument and small-computer market. The company split up into small, relatively autonomous divisions that were able to generate their own resources and make their own business decisions. It became a company policy to keep division size to about 1,000 employees; if a division gets significantly larger than this, the company considers spinning off a separate unit.

Some companies shed all functions that are not a part of their core business—for example, support functions such as secretarial services, reprographic services, payroll and other human resource systems. Instead of performing these functions in house, they contract with external suppliers—rather as a smaller company would.

Other companies restructure into teams that have enough autonomy to enable them to respond to customers' concerns quickly and effectively.

For example, New United Motors (NUMMI) has teams that are responsible for sections of the assembly line. Each worker can stop the line if he or she feels this is necessary to correct a problem. Each team is responsible for its production and quality and keeps track of its performance. Each team member learns every task so he or she can cover for one another. There are specialists in the company available to help the teams track down particularly difficult or unusual problems.

SPAN OF CONTROL

The question of what is a proper span of control has been much debated through the years. A ratio of five workers to one supervisor was proposed by the "scientific management" theorists of the 1930s and until recent times a span of five to seven has been seen as ideal. In the last 10 years or so, however, this supposed ideal has been challenged as being far too narrow. The emphasis today is on broadening spans of control so as to flatten organizations.

Before we go further, let's stop to see what difference it makes to have a relatively narrow or broad span of control.

With a narrow span of control:

◇ Cost of management is greater—simply because there are more managers for a given number of workers.

◇ Everything else being equal, with fewer workers to supervise, each manager has more time and energy for managerial duties and for nonmanagerial work.

◇ With closer supervision, workers get more individual attention and support from the boss, but also have less autonomy and less opportunity for self-direction.

◇ There are likely to be more levels of hierarchy with the accompanying features of a tall structure—such as slower communication and more difficulty coordinating among work groups.

With a broad span of control:

◇ Costs of management are lower.

◇ The supervisory task is more difficult, because managers have to spread their efforts among more workers. This means that other ways must be found to handle coordination, communication and other work that the company relies on managers to do.

◇ Workers are encouraged to develop skill and initiative; they have more opportunity to exercise their own judgment in making decisions about their work. This is a major source of job satisfaction for many people.

◇ To the extent that broader spans result in fewer organization levels, there is more direct communication between people at the lowest and highest levels of the organization.

◇ On the downside, workers who need or want close support from the boss are less likely to get it.

You can see that the nature of the work as well as the skill and experience of nonmanagerial employees come into play in deciding span of control. Another point to consider is that many "working supervisors" have considerable responsibility apart from supervision. For example, a sales manager might directly handle a number of customer accounts and have only a small amount of time to supervise other sales personnel. Or an engineer might work on projects along with other engineers he supervises. For these people, a narrow span of control might be quite appropriate.

Summary of Span of Control

Here is a summary of the preceding points.

A *narrow span* might be most appropriate in cases:

• Where the work to be supervised is complex and unpredictable

• Where the work of all the people in the group has to be closely coordinated

- Where workers are unskilled or inexperienced
- Where the manager is expected to perform other work in addition to supervision

By contrast, a *broad span* might be most appropriate where:

- The work is straightforward
- There are standard rules and procedures to guide workers
- Workers are highly capable and experienced
- Other sources of support, such as staff experts, are available
- Relatively autonomous work groups, such as business process teams, are used

CENTRALIZATION AND DECENTRALIZATION

We now come to the important issue of who makes what kind of decisions and controls what kind of resources. As we said earlier, when we talk about organizations as centralized or decentralized we are referring to how concentrated or dispersed is the authority to make decisions. Today, most organization experts say decisions should be made as far down in the organization and as close to the customer as possible, making for maximum responsiveness to customer needs. This implies decentralization. Many of today's successful companies take this philosophy to heart.

> *For example, Hewlett-Packard in the 1980s had 38 central committees that ruled most major aspects of its business. This structure slowed down the company's ability to react to changes in their competitive environment. Recognizing this, in 1990 the company dissolved these committees and decentralized most of the authority to the divisions.*

In spite of this, as you will read time and again in today's business press, other large companies appear to be doing the opposite; that is, they are centralizing functions that were formerly decentralized. And they have good reasons for doing so. One example of this is given in the "Western Electricity & Gas" case study.

In fact, organizations commonly swing from centralized to decentralized and back again as their circumstances change and priorities alter.

Case Study:
Western Electricity & Gas:
Centralization or Decentralization?

Western Electricity & Gas is a large state-regulated utility company in the western United States. Some years ago, the company decided to decentralize in order to be more responsive to customers at the local-division level. As a result, local divisions were given increased decision-making authority over several functions that formerly were tightly controlled by corporate head office. Two of these functions were human resources and transmission maintenance.

The reorganization called for a human resources department to be set up in every division. Division managers were delighted because this meant they could get timely action on local personnel issues, which in turn resulted in better service to customers. The downside, of course, was the fact that many more human resource employees were needed to staff all the new division human resource units, thus greatly increasing the cost of this function. Now, the company is facing a lot of pressure to lower its rates, and the costs of decentralizing are seen as far outweighing the benefits. Accordingly, the human resources function is being recentralized, with accompanying major reductions in staff size.

In the case of transmission maintenance, Western Electricity & Gas is also moving toward recentralization. This is largely to enable the company to distribute maintenance dollars more effectively and efficiently across the total utility transmission system. When it recently compared its practices with other similar companies worldwide, Western found that companies that control transmission maintenance from a central place were able to prioritize work and spending to achieve maximum performance of the whole system.

Three Major Reasons to Centralize

* *Control*

Centralization is an organization's most sure-fire method of controlling and coordinating activity and resources. Central control is especially important:

   ◇ When the company as a whole has to meet legal or regulatory requirements that are difficult to interpret

   ◇ When decisions made at a local level will affect the whole company—for example, a local division's interpretation of the company's contract with a labor union will be binding on the whole company

   ◇ When what occurs in one part of the company will affect every other part—as would be the case with a company-wide system or network like the transmission system in a utility company

* *Cost*

Because of "economies of scale," a centralized function can generally be managed with fewer resources than a decentralized function.

Consider the purchasing function in a large company. With purchasing for the whole company done in a central department, the company can get better quantity discounts than would be available to any one division of the company. Any time a large number of similar tasks are performed in one place, "economies" are possible because equipment and facilities can be shared, and generally fewer people are needed to do the work (as in the case of Western's human resources function).

* *New Technology*

Over recent decades, the rate of technological change has been phenomenal. New technology enables many a decentralized company to centralize, and vice versa.

Another way in which Western Electricity & Gas has centralized its operations is by reducing the number of its customer call centers from 24 to four. This has not only resulted in lower costs of operation, but because of new telephone technology, has produced faster response to customers. When there is high demand in one center, as in the case of a major power outage, calls are automatically routed to one of the other centers. Thus, new technology has permitted centralization of a function to be both more efficient and more effective in serving customers.

Three Major Reasons to Decentralize

• *Responsiveness*

With decision making pushed down to a local level, the company can respond more quickly to customers and local conditions.

• *Independence*

Decentralization tends to stimulate creativity and independence in people at lower levels and helps build a pool of candidates for higher-level positions.

• *New Technology*

New computer technology enables companies to decentralize authority to a much greater extent than was previously possible. One of the main reasons for centralizing authority is to ensure that top management knows about and can influence what is happening throughout the organization. Today's sophisticated information systems enable authority to be delegated to lower levels while still keeping top management well informed.

Factors to Consider in Centralizing or Decentralizing

Here is a good rule of thumb to follow.

> *Make sure decisions are made by people who are as close as possible to the source of information and the field of action; this way, you will get quicker and better informed decisions. Yet, recognize that some decisions may have to be centralized for the good of the total organization.*

In some large organizations, there is a formal *delegation of authority* system, which specifies who gets to make what decisions. This is an issue that needs to be considered carefully. Some factors to take into account in delegating authority include:

- *Duration*

How far into the future does the decision commit the organization? How fast can it be reversed?

Generally speaking, the more long-term the decision and the more difficult it is to reverse, the higher level decision makers need to be.

- *Impact*

What is the effect of the decision on other departments or divisions or on the organization as a whole?

The more the decision affects the organization as a whole or other parts of the organization, the more senior decision makers need to be involved.

- *Cost*

What is the cost of implementing the decision? You need to take into account not only the cost of resources—like people, money, materials—but also more subtle factors such as possible loss of customer confidence or employee morale. What would it cost to reverse the decision and its consequences?

The higher the cost, the more senior-level decision makers will be involved.

Summary of Centralization and Decentralization

There are many different kinds of decisions that organizations make. Some are almost always made at the top level. These would include decisions that affect the company as a whole: its mission, overall budget, company goals and strategies, its policies on legal and ethical issues. Others are nearly always made at lower levels: evaluation of work quality, productivity of individual workers, specific actions to take and tasks to complete in the moment. But in many areas, there is a wide variation with some companies centralizing, others decentralizing, others decentralizing but with top-level guidelines or standards. Indeed, experimenting with this "centralization-decentralization" variable is a way that many organizations discover opportunities to cut costs and get a competitive advantage.

Table 3-2 lists examples of decisions that are typically made at different levels.

TABLE 3-2. Kinds of decisions that companies make.		
Kind of Decision	**Level of Management Who Makes Decision**	**Comments**
Companywide mission, strategy and goals	Top level	Sometimes with input from other levels
Policies on legal and ethical issues	Top level	
Legal and legislative issues	Top level	
Finance—issuing stock, floating bonds, getting bank loans	Top level	Sometimes profit centers handle their own
Mission of departments, divisions	Top level	Initially established by top but reviewed and revised by departments/divisions
Goals and strategies of divisions and departments	Division/department level	Often review and approval by top is needed
Products and services to offer	Sometimes top level Sometimes division/ department level	Varies greatly
Customers and markets to target and prices to charge	Sometimes top level Sometimes division/ department level	Varies greatly
Customer's special requests or complaints	Sometimes individual worker level Sometimes first-level supervisor Sometimes division/ department level	Top level only for very large customers
Allocation of money, people and other resources	Top level for company as a whole Lower levels for their own part of the organization	

(Table continues)

TABLE 3-2 (continued)

Kind of Decision	Level of Management Who Makes Decision	Comments
External relations—e.g., with government agencies	Top level for national issues Division/department or lower levels for local issues	
Workforce size ("headcount")	Division or department level	Top level if company is "downsizing" and a companywide workforce size policy is in effect
Human resource policies and practices—e.g., salaries, working conditions, education, training	Top level in large companies. Often at middle or lower management levels in small ones	
Work assignment to individuals	First-level supervisor	
Work quality and quantity	First-level supervisor	
Work procedures—how to do the work	Sometimes individual worker level Sometimes first-level supervisor Sometimes division/department level Sometimes top level	Middle and top level may set goals and standards When middle and top level decide work procedures, these are distributed through policy and procedure manuels

PUTTING IT ALL TOGETHER

As you can see, the three factors of span of control, levels of hierarchy and centralization or decentralization of decisions are often interrelated. Narrow spans tend to accompany tall structures and centralized decision making. Broad spans tend to go with flat structures and decentralized decision making. These broad generalizations apply much of the time, but there certainly are exceptions as the following example shows.

Western Electricity & Gas, as mentioned earlier, has recently centralized many functions that were previously decentralized. This was in response to a need to cut costs. At the same time, in another cost-cutting move, the company eliminated an entire layer of management by removing the regional level that formerly oversaw the operations of local divisions. Those divisions now report directly to the corporate headquarters. This is an example of a company that flattened *its organization structure while* centralizing *many formerly decentralized functions.*

GUIDELINES FOR CREATING MANAGEMENT STRUCTURE

Perhaps the most important piece of advice we can offer is, don't let it "just happen." All too often management structure is not the result of careful thought and planning, but rather a consequence of other changes. For example, changes in workforce size—up or down—often leave managers with much broader or narrower spans of control than they had before.

Or, as in the Beaumont Machining example given earlier, a top manager appoints a middle manager to relieve the load on the top, and this has the "ripple effects" of an extra level. These include changing people's work responsibilities, communication patterns and what sorts of decisions they make.

In reviewing your management structure, think about the intended and unintended consequences of the number of levels of hierarchy, the spans of control and the levels at which decisions are made. The following examples show these can affect your goals, key success factors and business processes.

> One of Western Electricity's core business processes is the new business process. Typically, at the first step in this process a developer requests the company to design and install electric and gas facilities for a new subdivision. The process involves planning, estimating, engineering, construction and final installation of service. After the company's regions were eliminated, the local divisions had control over all steps of the new business process. This meant customers could get faster and more responsive service than they did when all decisions had to be approved by the region.

> In the Mail Room example described earlier, the department was plagued by poor performance. The extra level of supervision they added resulted in narrower spans of control, which has helped them achieve their goals of raising production and reducing complaints about misdirected mail.

Who Should Be Involved?

◊ ***People at higher levels.*** A level of management is typically added or eliminated as a result of a decision made by the level above it. This is because some strain felt by the higher level managers is creating the perceived need for change.

> *At Beaumont Machining, the higher-level person (Bill Beaumont) experienced work overload that was relieved by creating a supervisory level in the machine shop. In the case of PSI, top management wanted to cut costs, and eliminating the regional level was one way to do this.*

◊ ***People at lower levels who are affected.*** Whoever makes the decision, it is valuable to get input from everyone who would be directly affected by such a move.

> *In the Beaumont Machining case, Bill Beaumont met first with Manuel to get his reactions to his proposal to make Manuel a supervisor over the other machinists. Then, he and Manuel held a meeting of all machinists. Manuel's new role was explained and the machinists were asked for their questions and reac-tions. As a result, many issues about people's responsibilities were clarified. It was explained under what circumstances a machinist could approach Bill directly rather than going through Manuel. By having this discussion up front, the new structure worked smoothly from the start.*

◊ ***Others inside or outside the company.*** Creating or removing a level of management is likely to affect relationships with other departments inside the company and with customers and suppliers outside the company. You may not wish to involve these people in the decision to add or remove a level, but it is important to communicate the change to anyone whose business relationship would be affected, to answer their questions and address their concerns.

Ways to Gather Information

It may be difficult for a manager or a design team by themselves to answer the questions on the worksheet. Some ways to gather information are by:

Observing—See what is happening in terms of results.

Asking people—Get the views of people at different levels of the organization and, if appropriate, people outside the organization such as customers and suppliers.

Experimenting—For example, when a supervisory position is vacant, the manager might try having subordinates report directly to the former supervisor's boss and then ask questions about what worked well and what didn't.

Benchmarking—Find out what other companies do in similar circumstances.

Reading and research—What have been the experiences of others in your own or related industries?

Remember: It is essential that decisions on management structure benefit the company in terms of your key success factors and serving your business processes. Think especially about customer satisfaction, product timeliness and quality, costs of production and company profitability, employee satisfaction and development.

Worksheet

Answering the following questions for each part of the organization you're designing will help you to think through your own situation.

Levels of Hierarchy

1. **How many levels of management do you have in your present or proposed organization?** (Remember, the number of levels might be different in different parts of your organization.)

   _____

   _____

2. **What are the costs and benefits to the company as a whole of having each level of management?** To each manager or supervisor? To the workers reporting to each manager?

   _____

   _____

   _____

3. **Thinking in terms of your goals, business processes and key success factors: Are there places where it might be desirable to eliminate a level of management?** What would be the possible drawbacks or benefits of doing this? How would the work formerly done by the managers at that level be handled?

   _____

   _____

   _____

4. **Are there places where it might be beneficial to add a level of management?** What value would it contribute to the organization? What might be the downsides of doing this, and can they be overcome?

_____

_____

_____

Spans of Control

5. **What is the span of control for each of the managers and supervisors in your organization?**

_____

_____

_____

6. **Do any of these seem to warrant investigation?** (Suggestion: look first at spans of four or less and spans of 10 or more.)

_____

_____

_____

7. **Describe any problems you have noted that might be due to an overly narrow or overly broad span.**

_____

_____

_____

8. **Might it make sense to consider changing the span of control in particular cases?** What do the managers and supervisors involved think?

_____

_____

_____

9. **Will changing spans of control lead to more or fewer levels of hierarchy?** If so, what would be the "ripple effects" of this?

_____

_____

_____

10. **If you're broadening spans of control, what are your plans to change the expectations and skills of managers and workers so they can work successfully with the new span?** What else needs to change to make the new span work?

_____

_____

_____

Decision Making

11. **What kinds of decisions can be made and actions taken at each level in your organization?**

_____

_____

_____

12. **Are there some decisions that could be delegated to lower levels?**

_____

_____

_____

13. **What would be the consequences of doing this in specific cases in terms of your goals, business processes and success factors?**

_____

_____

_____

14. **What additional knowledge and skills will be needed for employees at lower levels to make these decisions?** How would people's roles and jobs change?

_____

_____

_____

15. **What decisions _must_ be centralized at the top level of the organization, and why?**

_____

_____

_____

Chapter Four

COORDINATION

AND

CONTROL

Once structures are in place for dividing up and managing the work, you need techniques for ensuring that activities are coordinated and the right work gets done in the right way.

This chapter describes four techniques for coordinating and controlling work.

◇ Supervision

◇ Standardization

◇ Building employee commitment

◇ Teams

It also includes guidelines for selecting your own techniques.

The whole point of creating structure is to divide up work into manageable units and make it clear who is responsible for what. You now need to decide on techniques for:

1. *Coordinating* the work—that is, integrating the activities of different people working to produce the same end product or service.

2. *Controlling* the work—that is, making sure people are doing what they need to be doing and are doing it in the right way.

3. *Measuring* performance—that is, finding out to what extent you are reaching your goals and targets.

This chapter describes techniques for coordinating and controlling work, and presents guidelines for selecting your own techniques. Performance measurement is covered in Chapter 5.

COORDINATION AND CONTROL TECHNIQUES

In practice, the two activities of coordinating and controlling overlap; the very act of coordinating implies that some control is occurring. For this reason, we discuss them together. However, it is possible to coordinate using one technique and to control using another, as we'll discuss.

There are four basic techniques that organizations use to make sure that work is coordinated and controlled. Commonly, you'll find all methods used within the same company. Different companies, or different departments within the same company, may tend to use one method more than others in certain situations. Some may lean toward one method to coordinate work and another to control work. The four techniques are:

1. Supervision

2. Standardization

3. Building employee commitment

4. Teams

1. Supervision

A supervisor coordinates by establishing priorities and schedules, assigning people to tasks, making sure that interdependent activities are correctly timed. In addition to integrating the work efforts of people within the unit, the supervisor also helps to link the work of the whole unit to other units in the company.

A supervisor exercises control (a) through monitoring workers' behavior—for example, watching and directing them as they work, and/or (b) by examining finished work and instructing workers to make corrections if warranted.

It is possible to use supervision to coordinate but not control work, as the following example shows:

At Beaumont Machining, the new supervisor, Manuel, carries out many traditional supervisory tasks such as assigning work and preparing work schedules. However, each machinist is fully trained and typically completes each assignment without needing to consult Manuel. Control over each machinist's work occurs through the use of standard operating procedures and specifications set for the final product. (See the discussion of standardization of process and outcomes later in this chapter.) In other words, Beaumont uses Manuel primarily to coordinate rather than control work.

Contrast the above case with the situation of telephone operators whose supervisors both coordinate and control their work.

Telephone operators are arranged at computer consoles in a room with a supervisor observing them, keeping track of the amount of time each is spending per call, and sometimes listening in to monitor conversations. Information operators are expected to take an average of no more than six seconds per call. If an operator needs to take a break, he or she must signal the supervisor and get permission before leaving the station.

This is an example of supervision used to control performance. Supervisors watch what the workers are doing and how they're doing it and give immediate feedback on performance. These supervisors also coordinate work by planning schedules, arranging for replacements to take the place of absent workers, and so on.

Supervision and Spans of Control

The shape of the management structure we discussed in the last chapter has an effect on the extent to which supervision is a feasible means of control. In cases where the structure is flat and spans of control are broad, supervisors may still coordinate activities, but the company must use other methods to control what work is done and how it is done. Where the structure is tall and spans are narrow, supervision is feasible for both control and coordination.

When to Use Supervision

Besides span of control, there are several other factors that affect how appropriate it is to use supervision as a primary coordination and/or control method. In general, supervision is a good option to consider when:

◇ Interdependence among the positions supervised is high.

◇ The supervisor has special knowledge about the work that workers do not share.

◇ Timing is critical and having close supervision is the best way to ensure it.

◇ Errors could be costly—for example, when the work is dangerous.

◇ The work is complex and unpredictable, and workers lack the knowledge, experience or motivation to make decisions about the exceptions to routine that arise.

The following example of supervision as a good alternative illustrates most of these points.

A small research group of highly specialized technical experts is designing a component for a nuclear reactor. Each expert is a specialist on one aspect of the work: mechanical, electrical, nuclear, regulatory requirements. The work of the individuals is highly interdependent—that is, if one person produces poor quality work, it will jeopardize the whole enterprise. The supervisor of the group, unlike the other members, has built similar devices before and understands well how the different pieces of work will fit together and how the finished component will fit into the overall reactor assembly. He supervises the group fairly closely in terms of setting priorities, assessing work quality of individuals, ensuring timing and quality are on target and advising individuals of what needs to be changed in the event their work does not measure up.

This supervisor adds value to the team and to the company because he understands the work that each specialist does and how it contributes to the whole. He understands what the whole must look like and has experience in timing and prioritizing such work projects.

Contrast the above situation with the following one where supervisors seem to be superfluous.

A catalog sales company has 12 customer service clerks. There are four supervisors, each supervising three clerks. The supervisors report to a customer services manager. Procedures for handling customer calls are fairly routine. There is little interdependence among the tasks; each clerk typically can respond to a customer without needing to coordinate with the other clerks. Most of the clerks have held their jobs for many years and seldom have to ask their supervisor for help. The supervisors handle administrative matters such as vacation scheduling. They also, according to the clerks, tend to think up "busy work" for everyone to do because they themselves are not fully occupied.

These supervisors seem to add little value to the company—their subordinates know the work; the department manager could easily handle the few unusual problems that arise. Eliminating the four positions would probably result in a more efficient operation and increased job satisfaction for the clerks.

Potential Drawbacks of Using Supervision to Control

Whether or not your situation warrants using supervision to control work, there are some potential negative consequences.

◇ Employee creativity and initiative may be stifled, especially if the supervisor tends to monitor their actions closely.

◇ Workers may learn to deny personal responsibility for their work and instead rely on the supervisor to catch mistakes.

◇ Employees may put more effort into keeping their supervisor happy than in trying to satisfy the customer.

◇ If the supervisor's expertise and experience are no greater than those of the employees, he/she may not have credibility when trying to monitor and correct their work.

2. Standardization

The second major technique used to coordinate and control is standardization. This means setting standards and criteria to make sure that events follow a predictable path and produce predictable outcomes. It is possible to standardize:

- *Work process,* or how things are done
- *Outcomes* of the work, such as products and services
- *Inputs* to the work, such as the credentials of employees and the quality of materials and equipment

Standardizing Process

Standardizing process simply means having rules or procedures or policies that specify how things are to be done.

The assembly line, as it was originally conceived, is a perfect example of an attempt to standardize a work process. Often, the "what, when, and how" of every step in the assembly process was specified in detail down to the number of hand and arm movements and footsteps to take.

Nearly all organizations standardize some processes to some degree, but seldom to the extent of the assembly line described. In fact, today even assembly lines are not so rigid; workers typically have more discretion in terms of rotating tasks and taking action to ensure quality—sometimes even stopping the line if they think it necessary.

Process rules might be communicated verbally and informally. The new order clerk is told: "Every time you get an order for A-type widgets, give it to Joe. Give orders for B-type widgets to Sally."

Or there might be hefty policy manuals and standard operating procedures that spell out every step of every work process. In some cases, employees are sent to training classes to learn how to do their jobs. Many trades have long apprenticeship periods before workers are considered sufficiently skilled to function as journeymen.

When to Use Standardization of Work Process

Standardization of work processes may be *useful:*

- If the work is routine, with few exceptions to the rules

- If demands for the product or service are predictable

- As an alternative to supervision when span of control is broad

- If workers' activities are visible and measurable

Standardization of work processes may be *essential* when:

- the customer or an external agency has specified procedures that must be followed (as is often the case in military or other govern-ment contracts)

  and/or

- the way things are done is critical to how they come out.

For example, in constructing a new building, each step from foundation to roof has to follow procedures to meet local government building codes. Furthermore, if the cement for the foundation is not mixed in the right way, laid in the right way and allowed to set for the right time, the resulting foundation may not have the strength to hold the building.

Potential Drawbacks of Standardizing Work Process

◇ Many people find it boring and demoralizing to have no control over how they do their work. They may withdraw their attention and lose enthusiasm, and work quality and productivity may suffer.

◇ Employees who are instructed to follow detailed process steps are less likely to think of ways to improve the process—and over time there is room for improvement in almost every process.

◇ It is also entirely possible to "standardize" error or waste into a process, leading to inferior quality and inefficiency.

Standardizing Outcomes

Standardizing outcomes means specifying that final results must meet certain standards or criteria. Sometimes, companies rely on outcomes alone to coordinate and control work. Consider the following situation.

The sales representatives working for a company that makes food-loading conveyors spend most of their time in the field. To be successful in their work, these representatives have to understand the customer's situation and recommend the most appropriate equipment; often, this equipment is tailored for the customer. They are skilled engineers as well as salespeople.

These employees cannot be supervised in person, nor is it a good idea to specify what steps they have to follow in doing their job. On the contrary, it is in the company's interests for them to be creative and flexible. Therefore, the company can best control performance by looking at the outcomes of their work: for example, the number of conveyors sold, new customers brought in, customer satisfaction ratings, or profit made for the company.

When Should Outcomes Not Be Standardized?

It is always appropriate—in fact, it is essential—to make clear what results are expected from work activity. All companies have, or should have, goals to be met. However, it's not always desirable to be too specific about what kind of results you're holding employees to. This would be the case when the outcome itself is not clear—for example, when developing a new product or trying to break new ground.

> *A software engineer in an entertainment software company has the task of developing a new computer game. The development group is virtually "cut loose" in order to work on this. Results expected are stated very broadly: that it be a game that customers will buy and that can be produced at a profit. Being bright and creative people, members of the design team are more likely to benefit the company by being given the freedom to experiment, perhaps make some false starts and develop a final product whose parameters they simply didn't know when they started out.*

Note that the expected results aren't left entirely open-ended. The expectation is that the product will sell and can be produced at a profit. But the company is willing to tolerate some false starts, and not to specify price, quantity, quality, target market and other criteria they might normally set in advance for finished products.

The above two examples illustrate the following general statements about standardizing outcomes.

Consider standardizing outcomes rather than standardizing process or using supervision, when:

◇ Span of control is too broad for supervision to be a good alternative

◇ Interdependence is low

◇ Outcomes are visible and measurable

◇ The supervisor is not as knowledgeable as the worker concerning how to do the work

◇ Workers are sufficiently experienced, skilled and dedicated to the company's success to be trusted to do the work the right way

◇ The organization wishes to encourage worker initiative and creativity

Don't be too specific about the outcomes expected when:

◇ Management has only a very general idea of what the final product will be so it is difficult to specify outcomes ahead of time, and

◇ The company can afford to use resources in an exploratory or developmental project, such as in the software company example above.

Standardizing Inputs

Another way that companies control work is by making sure that the resources that go into the work meet certain criteria. These resources include the knowledge and skills of people employed to work on a job, as well as tools, materials, equipment and so on.

Standardizing People

There are many positions that companies fill by hiring unskilled workers. The fast food industry is a classic example. But, in other cases—and these are increasing as work becomes more complex— organizations rely heavily on recruiting employees who already have special skills and experience.

Sometimes, the new employees will be the only ones in the organization with those special skills. In these cases, it's difficult for company management to control through supervision, or by standardizing processes or outcomes—at least initially. So, instead, they rely heavily on the qualifications of the people they hire: academic or technical training, experience, references from former employers and so on. For example:

Some years ago, a research and consulting firm in California acquired computers for data analysis. Previously, data analysis work had been performed by an outside contractor. Although

the company contracted with the vendor to install and maintain the hardware, they found they needed to hire computer programmers to set up their databases and develop the necessary programs. At first, it was difficult for them to know how to set standards for or to evaluate the work of these programmers— no one else in the company, including their supervisor, was computer literate. Over time, of course, this situation was resolved as some programmers turned out to be more competent than others and company managers learned how to evaluate programming work.

Standardizing Materials and Equipment

Companies also standardize inputs by setting standards and specifications for goods and services purchased from suppliers. In some cases, there might also be some physical inspection of the goods, especially with a new supplier or one that hasn't lived up to its commitments in the past.

One of the primary strategies of *total quality management* is to establish minimum standards for parts and require suppliers to meet these standards. There is a quality certification process called ISO 9000 that establishes a whole set of requirements for relationships with suppliers that organizations seeking to be officially designated "world class" must meet.

3. Building Employee Commitment

A third coordination and control technique is to have employees who are so dedicated to the success of the organization that they can be relied on to do the best work possible and cooperate fully with others to make sure desired results are achieved.

This commitment must not be blind. It must be based on an understanding of the organization's business situation and strategies, its problems and opportunities and the way the employee can contribute to its success. Also, to be fully motivated, the individual must see some overlap between company goals and personal goals.

The idea of commitment based on shared goals and values is at the heart of the interest in corporate culture as a potential competitive advantage. Corporate culture refers to the set of beliefs, values and behaviors that characterize an organization.

To a great extent, the realization that corporate culture could provide competitive advantage came from studies of Hewlett-Packard. Hewlett-Packard developed a way of doing business called the "HP Way." The HP Way refers to the basic principles of encouraging and supporting individual creativity and initiative, freedom of action to achieve both personal and company goals, building the highest value products, treating people well and sharing the rewards of success. The HP Way provides guidelines and support for employees to contribute their best efforts even in unfamiliar situations.

It is becoming increasingly recognized that an employee's commitment to the success of the organization is a critical success factor. Approaches like employee involvement, continuous improvement and total quality are all based on:

◇ The premise that the people who do the work know the most about it and are the best source of ideas for improvement

◇ The idea that commitment to the company's success is critical in helping it beat the competition

Very few organizations rely solely on employee commitment to achieve coordination and control. However, some rely on it quite heavily as the following examples illustrate.

A nonprofit organization example is that of the Bayshore Humane Society in Northern California. This has a large volunteer force and a small paid staff. Staff members are underpaid, compared with similar positions elsewhere, and work hard, often long hours. They are passionately dedicated to animal welfare, sometimes make up the rules as they go along and have little supervision. The organization trusts that they will do the best possible job because all share a common dedication to their cause.

A typical for-profit organization example is that of a Silicon Valley start-up computer company. This company began with only "seat-of-the-pants" procedures to guide them because no one really knew how to run such a company. They eventually succeeded largely because the employees were enthusiastic and totally committed to the organization's success. They were motivated by the prospects of a good financial future in the long run, and this together with the excitement and challenge intrinsic in their work compensated for the confusion, long hours and lack of job security in the short term.

Commitment and the Employee

As we said earlier, commitment to the organization depends at least in part on some perceived overlap between the individual's goals and the organization's goals. There are many other factors that characterize an organization with a high degree of employee commitment.

Factors That Increase Commitment

- **Inspiring Mission and Shared Values.** Values are deeply held beliefs about what is good and desirable. Some employees are drawn to a company because of its mission and values.

  For example, the volunteers and staff of the humane society just mentioned passionately value the humane treatment of animals. They are also dedicated to achieving its mission—which is to rescue, provide medical treatment for, and try to find homes for stray animals within the county; and to educate the public on animal welfare.

- **Visionary Leadership**. Inspiring leaders can communicate the organization's mission and values in a way that motivates employees to follow. Visionary leaders project an image of the future that arouses energy and enthusiasm in their followers.

- **Shared Glory and Sacrifice.** This means employees share the rewards when things go right, and everyone, including top management, shares the sacrifice when the organization isn't doing so well.

- **Employees Are Involved.** Employees at all levels are involved in setting goals, planning the work and solving problems that arise. Employee suggestions are taken seriously, and there are reasonable explanations for suggestions that are turned down.

- **Employees Know How They're Doing.** Performance results are shared so that employees know how they personally, the unit and the whole organization are doing. Good work is acknowledged and rewarded.

- **Employees Understand Where They Fit.** Employees understand how their part of the work fits with other parts and how it links to the end product or service. Some organizational experts believe that a broad scope of work and a high degree of employee control over how it's done also contribute to a high degree of commitment.

- **Managers Are Good Communicators.** People are more likely to be influenced by their immediate supervisor than by any other form of communication in the company. Managers and supervisors who are dedicated to the company's success have a powerful impact in shaping the attitudes of employees.

Factors That Erode Commitment

- **Lack of Job Security.** Commitment is perceived as a two-way street. When job security is threatened, and especially if this happens often, people start to question the organization's commitment to its employees.

- **Management Incompetence.** Perceived evidence of incompetent, arbitrary or unethical behavior in managers decreases employee trust in the organization.

- **Management Isn't "Walking the Talk."** This is the perception that others in the organization, especially top management, are not themselves doing what they expect other employees to do.

Too Much Reliance on Employee Commitment

- **Underorganization.** Organizations that rely very heavily on employee commitment may pay too little attention to structure and procedures. As a result, the organization is not as efficient or as effective as it might be.

- **Overidentification.** Employees sometimes become too identified with the organization. Their high degree of commitment results in their becoming "burned out" in its service.

- **Opposition Is Silenced.** When employees are strongly bound together in pursuit of a common cause, it's difficult for anyone to disagree with the organization's direction and ways of doing things. Dissidents are pressured into accepting the status quo, or they may leave the organization. This means that if change becomes necessary due to a changing business environment, the organization is slow to react.

4. Teams

As we read and hear every day in the news media, the world of business is changing at an ever-accelerating pace. Often, traditional methods of coordinating work—like supervision and standardization—simply aren't enough to get the fast changes and quick results needed to survive and thrive in today's environment.

Work teams designed to fit the requirements and opportunities of particular business settings are frequently the answer. Teams are especially useful when there is a need for flexibility and speed in handling work and when it's important to have input from different parts of the organization simultaneously.

In Chapter 2 we described a type of organization structure that is based on business process teams. However, there are many different kinds of teams and they can be found in all types of organizations: functional, product-based, customer-based and matrix.

The business process teams we described in Chapter 2 are relatively permanent in nature. Other teams have a very limited life span, being pulled together to accomplish a specific task and then disbanded. Some teams are relatively informal, meeting occasionally to resolve unusual problems that arise. Some are added to the employees' regular duties, like continuous improvement teams or quality circles. Others are very high profile, charged with major one-time tasks that are "life or death" for the company.

Teams vary considerably not only in the scope of work assigned to them and its potential impact, but also in the extent to which the team itself rather than someone else in the company establishes goals, allocates resources and is held responsible for results. Some examples:

◇ A construction crew is a team. Its scope of responsibility is limited, and typically its work has little impact outside the group. It has little control over the resources assigned to it or its work assignments.

◇ Another kind of team is a project team. Sometimes the team leader estimates and requests resources for the project; sometimes he or she can specify who will be on the team. Projects vary in terms of their budget, complexity of the work, length of time to complete, size of the team. Usually some higher level of management sets the goals and defines the scope of the work.

◇ A self-managed (or semi-autonomous) work team is one that has considerable authority to make all decisions regarding the team: selection of members, how to do the work, setting team goals and how to use the money allocated to them. Business process teams may fall into this category.

Teams coordinate work because by its nature a team is a group of highly interacting people who cooperate to produce common outcomes. The members see and talk to each other as they work together, and each individual consciously adjusts his or her own activities when needed to mesh with the work of other team members.

Control is achieved in teams because the visible nature of each team member's work both (a) motivates people to meet the team's expectations of performance and (b) provides ample opportunity for other team members to suggest changes. Peer approval and disapproval are powerful influences in leading people to meet expectations.

Teams are especially valuable if:

◇ You need the input and collaboration of people representing different departments, professional or technical disciplines and points of view.

◇ Interdependence among tasks is high.

◇ You would like to have people "cross-trained" in different skills and abilities. Working on a team, for example, can help a design engineer and a sales representative understand each other's problems and opportunities.

◇ The challenges you face are too complex for any one person either to meet or to evaluate a response proposed by someone else.

◇ Direct interaction among individuals is the fastest and most effective way to coordinate the pieces of work in a project or process.

◇ You want to encourage employee participation.

A team *works best* when:

◇ Team members are sufficiently skilled and experienced to do the work and make the necessary decisions.

◇ Team members have the "human relations" skills to work well together and are willing to set aside individual preferences when necessary to get results.

◇ It receives clear goals and direction from management; generally, these should relate to expected results, not to team process.

◇ After making expectations clear, management is willing to trust in the team—to give it time to get established and to provide support when things don't go as planned.

Team Spirit

Much has been written about team spirit—that feeling of dedication to the team and enthusiasm about reaching its goals.

Team spirit can be wonderful when:

◇ It helps highly productive people produce high-quality goods and services.

◇ It builds loyalty and commitment to the company as a whole.

◇ It makes people happy to come to work.

Team spirit is *not* so wonderful when:

◇ The team becomes more committed to its own goals than to the company's.

◇ "Groupthink" develops. It becomes difficult for an individual member to challenge the group, so dissent is silenced.

◇ Team members become blind to, or just refuse to acknowledge, one another's shortcomings. ("He's one of us so we won't criticize.")

These potential drawbacks can be addressed by having periodic changeover of team members; however, too frequent changes in membership can prevent or reduce cohesion in the team. The trick is to get a good balance of stability and change and to make sure that team members have access to new ideas and methods.

Points to Ponder

1. Think of a team you've been a part of that has achieved parti-cularly good results. Which of the organizational factors discussed above might have contributed to this?

2. How about a team that got poor results? What organizational factors might have led to its failure?

Management Style

Management style refers to the way that supervisors and managers interact with the employees who report to them. Style is an aspect of management behavior that has a big impact on how effective supervisors are likely to be in carrying out their duties. Management style can also affect and be affected by organization design.

Management styles range along a continuum from very high to very low control. At the one extreme, there is the militaristic "command and control" style where the boss calls the shots and workers have little to say about what or how work gets done.

At the other extreme, there is the completely "hands off" style where workers themselves decide what work needs to be done and how to do it. In between, there are styles with varying degrees of management control and worker involvement.

One well-known approach to leadership style (developed by Hersey and Blanchard, 1992) suggests that the appropriate management style moves among "telling," "selling," "participating," and "delegating." As you might guess:

Telling means directing and closely monitoring workers' activities.

Selling means explaining decisions and answering questions.

Participating means joining in discussion with workers to figure out what needs to be done and how.

Delegating means leaving decisions and implementation up to the workers.

Each of these styles involves significantly different behaviors and attitudes in supervisors and workers. In general, the more capable and mature workers are, the more supervisors can use the participation and delegation styles. Conversely, the less able and mature workers are, the more selling and telling styles are needed. Also, in general, the more support workers need to figure out and be motivated to do the work, the more participation and selling are appropriate.

Today, another kind of style is being stressed: the *coaching* or *developmental* style. With this approach, the supervisor's objective is to help people understand how best to get their work done; develop the knowledge, abilities and maturity to participate at a higher level; and become more independent or autonomous.

Historically, the telling and selling styles have been most common, especially when the organization used supervision or standardization of process as control techniques.

But times are changing. Competition is global today and the fast pace of change means that the organization can use all the help it can get from employees at all levels. Being responsive to customers and keeping costs low call for a unified effort—with cooperation, dedication and initiative on the part of every employee.

As a result, the participating, delegating and coaching styles are increasingly favored. These styles fit particularly well with the coordination and control techniques of standardized outcomes, teams and employee commitment. However, in practice, all the coordination and control techniques we describe can be used with the whole range of management styles.

Points to Ponder

Supervision as a control technique can be used with a variety of management styles. What situations are you aware of, in your organization or elsewhere, where supervisors with different management styles get quite different results?

Informal Organization

So far, we have discussed formal ways to coordinate and control work. But in fact, a lot of coordination and control occurs in quite informal and nonofficial ways. Workers often bypass official channels of communication and bend standard operating procedures. This is why it's important to be aware of how things are *actually* done in addition to knowing how they're *supposed* to be done.

Flouting the rules can be harmful if it occurs through ignorance, indifference or even deliberate insubordination.

> *For example, in the Mail Room case discussed earlier, workers often didn't follow the proper procedures because their supervisor was too busy to help them or to discipline malingerers. As a result, their work was slow and inaccurate.*

But there are many situations where employees ignore the rules because it is faster and more effective to do so.

In an engineering and construction company, the foreman on the construction site finds an error in one of the drawings. According to standard procedure, he should notify the construction superintendent, who will in turn contact the chief engineer, who will then direct the matter to the engineer who prepared the drawings. In actual fact, the foreman often simply does what he feels to be correct, or he bypasses the chain of command and contacts the responsible engineer directly. This way, the error can be speedily corrected.

Both the construction superintendent and the chief engineer know this sort of thing occurs and both turn a blind eye. If, however, a major problem were to develop—like faulty construction that resulted because the engineering error wasn't properly corrected—then all four parties concerned would be in trouble for not following procedures.

When you find that formal procedures are regularly ignored in certain situations, it's important to understand why.

If *formal* procedures appear to be appropriate, perhaps employees don't understand them or perhaps your current techniques for controlling work are not effective.

◇ If you rely on *supervision*, perhaps the supervisor is overspanned or needs coaching in how to manage people.

◇ If you use *standardized process* or *outcomes,* perhaps the standards aren't being clearly communicated. Maybe oral instructions need to be written. Or written manuals are poorly designed and worded. Maybe workers need some training.

If *informal* procedures seem to be more effective than formal ones:

◇ Involve employees in proposing new formal procedures.

◇ Review the proposed new procedures with people who will be affected by them—inside and outside the organization, including customers, if appropriate.

◇ If the new procedures meet with approval, implement them—at least on a trial basis.

You might also consider revisiting your coordination and control techniques. Maybe there are too many formal rules and procedures. Maybe employees should be allowed to exercise more discretion in how they do their work than they are formally permitted at present.

SUMMARY OF COORDINATION AND CONTROL TECHNIQUES

In summary, which coordination and control technique, or combination of techniques, is likely to work best depends on a number of factors including:

- How work is divided up into units

- Span of control

- How quick and flexible the organization must be in responding to customers

- Nature of the work—whether it is complex and unpredictable, or routine and predictable

- How interdependent the work is within a unit or among different units

- Characteristics of workers; for example, levels of skill and experience

- How visible and measurable work activities are

- Whether the supervisor has special expertise not shared by the workers, or workers have expertise not shared by their supervisors

- Whether the company is trying to stimulate creativity and initiative in its workers

GUIDELINES FOR CHOOSING COORDINATION AND CONTROL TECHNIQUES

Who Should Be Involved?

◇ *Managers and others who are held responsible for results.* In many cases, managers and supervisors may not have given much thought to how they make sure work is coordinated or controlled. Answering the questions below will help them decide if their current techniques are the most appropriate ones to use.

◇ *Employees at all levels.* Employees who do the work have useful information on how coordination and control actually occur. In fact, managers at higher levels sometimes aren't aware of the full extent of the informal ways in which work gets done. Workers can also give useful input concerning what they need to make sure work is progressing as it should.

Worksheet

Ask yourselves the following questions.

1. When do we use the following methods to coordinate work and/or control work?

Supervision _____

Standardizing process _____

Standardizing outcomes _____

Standardizing inputs _____

Employee commitment _____

Employee teams _____

2. Describe any problems that have arisen in your work situation due to the technique used.

_____

_____

_____

3. Are there informal coordination and control methods used that sometimes replace the formal methods? If so, should you consider *enforcing* the formal methods? How about *changing* the formal methods?

_____

_____

_____

4. **Think of your new organization structure (or one that you would like to implement). What would be the most appropriate techniques for coordinating and controlling work in different parts of your organization?** Keep in mind how the new structure may have changed spans of control, interdependencies, nature of the work, and so on.

_____

_____

_____

5. **For each change proposed in #4 above, think through a "what if" scenario, identifying the potential benefits and costs of making the change in technique.** (See the "What If" box for an example of this.)

6. **Before actually implementing changes, especially if they are major, be sure to get input from the people who are responsible for the results of the work as well as the people who do the work.**

"What If" Scenario

We'll say that a hypothetical telephone company is considering controlling operators by *outcomes* rather than through *supervision*. They propose using a computer to track all the information the supervisors currently monitor—for example, length of time spent per call, number of calls answered per day, and so on. Their analysis might look like the following.

Change being considered

- Use computer to track outcomes, eliminating the need for supervisors to monitor behavior.

Potential benefits

- Salary costs will be lower with supervisory positions eliminated.
- Operators will have a more comfortable work environment by not having supervisors constantly looking over their shoulders.
- Operators will develop more personal responsibility for keeping up good performance.

Potential drawbacks

- Although the computerized reports will be available every day, problems with operator performance will be discovered through analysis only after the fact.
- Some operators, particularly if they are inexperienced, may need the guidance of a supervisor when unusual situations arise.

Chapter Five

MEASURING PERFORMANCE

The purpose of measuring performance is to see whether you're getting the results you want and, if not, where corrections need to be made. People pay attention to what's being measured. Measurement can be both a motivator and a threat. Though often used to focus on instances of failure, some would argue that measurement is most powerful when used to focus on instances of success. Certainly, you'll get the most out of any performance measurement system if you spend at least as much time reinforcing good performance as trying to correct poor performance.

Performance measurement consists of four basic steps:

1. *Deciding* what to measure, and how often

2. *Setting standards* or criteria for performance

3. *Noting any deviations* from the standards

4. Determining when and how to *take corrective action*

WHAT TO MEASURE?

To repeat, people pay attention to what gets measured. So be sure to measure those results you really need to keep track of. To help you decide which these results are, think about your:

Goals—the concrete results you intend to accomplish within a certain time period

Key success factors—those things you must do on an ongoing basis to be successful

Business processes—key milestones in your business processes

Most companies have measures that relate to financial results, costs of production, quantity and quality of goods produced, individual employee performance and customer satisfaction. For example:

Beaumont Machining attracts and retains customers by promising high-quality work, not necessarily at the lowest price. They make a high margin of profit on each order. They measure performance on two critical success factors: (1) quality of the product (accurate machining, durable materials, attractive finish) and (2) timeliness—that is, meeting promised delivery dates. (They have other performance measures also.)

Enlok Windows, by contrast, faces a highly competitive market where they must often be willing to lower their profit in order to make a sale. Their goals and measures are related to (1) volume—that is, total sales per year, and (2) production costs per order. The more they can sell and the more they can keep costs down, the more profit they will make.

These are some of the most common aspects of performance that get measured, with examples of the kind of measures used for each.

- **Profitability:** This refers to how much money is made after expenses—or the extent to which revenues exceed costs.

  Measures: Net sales (total dollar amount of sales minus costs of producing the goods or services). Earnings per share of stock. Return on assets.

- **Competitiveness:** This is the extent to which your organization is succeeding against competitors.

  Measures: Percent of market share or your total volume of sales for a certain product as a percentage of total volume of sales for that product by all producers.

- **Efficiency:** This means accomplishing results with the least wasteful use of resources.

  Measures: Resources expended per unit of output. Processing time per unit produced. Average number of customers served or units produced per employee. Average length of downtime of machinery or facilities.

- **Effectiveness:** Being effective means doing the right things to meet your customer's needs.

  Measures: Number of repeat customers. Ratings on customer satisfaction survey where customers are asked what their needs are and to what extent your products and services meet these needs.

- **Quality:** This refers to meeting or exceeding specifications or requirements.

  Measures: Percentage of products meeting quality criteria. Number of customer kudos or complaints. Number of product rejects. Ratings on customer satisfaction survey.

- **Volume:** This refers to quantity of output.

  Measures: Number of products manufactured, shipped, sold. Number of customers served, projects completed.

- **Innovation:** This is the extent to which you produce new ideas or adapt old ideas to create profitable results.

  Measures: Number of patents obtained for products. Number of new products or services developed. Number of employee suggestions implemented. Amount of money saved through continuous improvement of work processes.

- ***Quality of Work Life:*** This refers to aspects of the work environment that are valued by employees.

    Measures: Ratings on employee satisfaction survey. Employee turnover and absenteeism rates. Number of workplace accidents.

Process or Outcomes?

Always measure outcomes—even when you don't want to be too specific as to what results should be. This would be the case, for instance, in a group trying to develop a new computer game.

It may also be valuable to take measurements at interim steps in the process. In fact, the total quality movement of the last few decades stresses the importance of doing things right the first time rather than having to redo them because the end product is flawed. One way to ensure this is to have inspections and measurements at different steps in the process.

> *In a company making a food packaging machine, for example, all the parts must be produced to tight specifications and with narrow tolerances. They are made separately (on different machinery by different people). If any one set of parts fails to meet specifications, the total assembly will be held up: First, because it must be determined which part is at fault, and, second, time will be lost while the faulty part is remachined. This company, therefore, tests the parts at each stage of production to ensure no rework will have to be done during the final assembly.*

Incidentally, note that measuring the process doesn't necessarily imply having a standardized process. Having a standardized process means workers are told how to perform each step of the task. In contrast, measuring the process means that results at various stages are specified and then measured.

In brief, measure process as well as outcome when:

◇ There is a clear connection between how each step in the process is done and the final outcome

◇ It is likely mistakes may be made along the way—because the process is particularly complicated or variable, workers are inexperienced and so on

◇ Getting interim measurements will enable you to make corrections early and avoid flaws in the final product or service

Points to Ponder

Employees sometimes find it threatening to have their work results measured. How might you overcome their fears?

SETTING STANDARDS FOR MEASUREMENT

Deciding *what* to measure is often considerably easier than deciding *how* to measure it and what an acceptable standard should be. For example, you may decide that you need to measure quality, and that one measure of good quality would be number of rejects. But what is an acceptable number of rejects? Is it realistic to expect zero rejects?

Beaumont Machining established "number of rejects" as a measure of quality and "number of times the promised delivery date is met" as a measure of timeliness. The company's desire is to get zero rejects and always meet every promised delivery date. However, for reasons that are often beyond its control, this is not always possible. So the supervisor and machinists jointly decided on the following minimum standards:

*   **Reject rate:** *less than 5%*

*   **Timeliness:** *promised delivery dates met for 80% of orders; within 48 hours for remaining orders.*

Performance is measured once a month. If standards are not met, the supervisor, workers and sometimes the owner also, meet to determine what is causing the problems and try to correct the situation.

Two important questions to ask are how often and under what conditions should you do the measurement. For example, it seems sensible to measure the quality of products by examining a few examples coming off one machine at the same time every day. However, when you do this, you tend to observe products under the same conditions every time—same workers, same hour of the shift, same machine, same amount of machine running time. It's unwise to assume that the measure of quality you get at this one time, on this one machine, will hold for all times and machines. So, to get an accurate overall picture, you need to measure quality at different times with different workers, different machines, and so on. The same point holds true for all measurements when you want to be able to draw general conclusions, whether about employees, products, services or customers.

Once you decide what aspects of performance to track, how to measure each and under what conditions, you can set up the actual measurement system. You need to answer such questions as: Who will do the measuring? How often? How will they keep track—through a log book, a computer program or other means? Who will compile and report the results?

Measuring Qualitative Data

It is fairly easy to find ways to measure something that can be *quantified*. It is relatively simple, for instance, to measure dollar value of goods sold in a given time period, number of telephone calls answered, number of customer complaints received, number of rejects, length of time to complete a task. It is not nearly so easy to measure *qualitative* aspects of performance, such as effective management style, the productivity of administrative employees or the creativeness of engineers, designers and others whose job it is to produce original ideas.

A common way to quantify an abstract concept, such as customer satisfaction, is to do a *survey.* This means, for example, you would ask customers to complete a questionnaire that asks them to rate how well you're doing on various dimensions. If the questionnaire is carefully developed to make sure that the really important aspects of service are covered, this can be a good solution.

It's difficult, however, to avoid introducing a subjective bias into the answers. Consider the following questions asked by one large company in their Quality of Service Evaluation, administered annually. (Customers were told to circle a number from 1 to 5, with 1 representing poor to 5 representing excellent.)

How do our services compare in terms of cost, quality, value and timeliness to those that could be purchased from other sources?

Please rate the courtesy, cooperation and professionalism of our service representative.

In the case of the first question, obviously the customer's response is going to be affected by how much experience the customer has had with other suppliers. Or the answers could be purely guesswork based on what the customer thinks other suppliers could provide. Similarly, the second question will be biased by the extent to which the person answering the question actually interacts with the service representative and likes him or her.

In spite of these shortcomings, the company feels that overly positive ratings tend to balance out overly negative ones, and that the results still give useful information on how customers view the service providers. Also, note that, while the survey is concerned with *qualitative* issues, the responses can be *quantified*. This makes it easy to track results over time and compare the results of one group with another.

ACTING ON RESULTS

Keeping in mind that measures are tools to help you improve performance, it is clear that what you do with the results is as important as deciding what and how to measure. Once the results are in, the next steps are to:

1. Determine what deviations occur—that is, where do results exceed or fall below what is expected.

2. Communicate the information to everyone involved in producing the results.

3. Use this information to reinforce good performance and correct poor performance.

If results *meet or exceed expectations,* be sure to acknowledge the workers responsible and, if appropriate, have them explain their success to other workers.

If results fall *below expectations,* you need to find out why. Focus on the problem itself, rather than trying to pin the blame on people. Don't punish people for telling the truth. We've all heard of situations where the boss has a tendency to "shoot the messenger" delivering bad news. This practice has two unfortunate consequences.

◇ Workers spend time and energy defending themselves from accusations of blame, rather than trying to understand and resolve the problem causing the poor performance.

◇ Workers are sometimes tempted to "fudge" the data to ensure that they have good results to report. For example, a bad run of widgets might get written off as an aberration and not be included in the day's numbers. Or only those customers who do a lot of business with the company, and thus get special treatment, are asked about their satisfaction with the company's services.

In both situations, measurement is not being used as the helpful tool it can be in improving performance.

No matter whether results exceed or fall short of standards, it's important to review the standards at regular intervals to see if they need to be revised. Sometimes this decision will be driven by your competition. For example, if a competitor starts to produce the same product you sell—at the same price but higher quality than you—you may have to raise your quality standards, even if your workers are finding it difficult to meet the current standards.

Communicating results, whatever they are, should be done frequently so that people know how they're doing as they go along. This enables problems to be corrected in a timely way. Many companies have an annual review of performance—both for individual workers and for the company as a whole. However, a year is a long time to wait to find out what's going well and what needs to be changed.

To be most effective, a *measurement-feedback-correction* cycle should be part of the work so that workers find it easy to check their performance regularly and be essentially self-correcting.

MEASUREMENT PITFALLS

Two major pitfalls to avoid are "measuring everything to death" and "over-concern with measurement."

Too Many Measures

This situation occurs when a company is too conscientious, and possibly too nonselective, in what it measures. It seems that everything that can be quantified is measured. Worse still, as yet more things need to be tracked, new measures are added without any of the old ones being dropped.

You can guess what happens. People stop being diligent about collecting the data, so often the resulting reports are inaccurate. As a result, those people who are supposed to monitor the results don't do it as much. If there are some conscientious people who really do track everything they're supposed to, they end up spending more time on measuring the work than in doing the work. Some suggestions on avoiding the "too many measures" pitfall are these.

◇ Concentrate on what's really important to the survival and growth of your business. Refer back to your goals, key success factors and business processes. Get input from your customers to help you set priorities.

◇ Don't give in to the temptation to measure something just because it's easy to measure. Measures of unimportant things dilute the attention paid to important things.

◇ Limit the number of things you measure. Some experts suggest having no more than 10 measures of performance.

Regularly, take a look at all the things you measure and ask: Why are we measuring this? Who actually uses the information, and how does it affect what our company does? Does anything change as a result? What would happen if we simply dropped this measure?

Overconcern with Measurement

Measurement is important, but it is not more important than being responsive to customers or doing the work well. As we illustrated earlier (with the Eastern utility company's quality program), it is possible for an organization, and for individuals, to become so carried away with racking up a high score on some aspects of performance that they overlook other—even more critical—aspects.

This situation is largely an unintended consequence of rewarding good performance! So, if an employee is rewarded for exceeding measurement standards on quality criteria, this is what he or she will focus on, and other nonmeasured aspects of performance may be ignored.

Consider the following case where a company's priorities changed during the course of the year.

> Among several goals set by a software company at the beginning of the year was one to develop a software product for a new market, the legal market. The company's existing and highly successful product is a software package for financial managers. Part way through the year, a competitor introduced a financial package that directly competes with its product. The major concern now becomes to meet this threat in every way it can: whether by adding new features to its financial package, cutting prices for new customers or providing better service for existing customers. The company still wants to develop a legal software package, but this is no longer as urgent a need as meeting the competitive threat for the accounting package.

Quite commonly, especially in large companies, when a situation like this occurs, the person or unit responsible for the legal package will still be held to the original goals. They will be measured on their success in achieving these goals. Thus, they will be reluctant to shift their priorities to focus time and resources on meeting the new threat unless the measures of success they are expected to meet are changed accordingly.

Here's a hypothetical example that illustrates a situation where what is *not* measured may be as important to the company in the long run as what *is*.

Two managers at year's end claim they have each achieved cost reductions of $15,000 during the year for their respective departments; quality of the work results remained the same. The managers received the same bonus for good performance.

Does this mean that the performance for the two departments is identical? Not necessarily. In one department, at year's end, employees expressed enthusiasm about their work, satisfaction with the company, their manager and the work environment. In the other department, dissatisfied employees were seeking employment elsewhere. Clearly, some things are working better in the first department than the second, and probably the manager of the first department is more effective than the manager of the second. But whatever the first manager is doing right is not being measured at present.

Points to Ponder

Because most organizations try to limit the number of performance measures, some aspects of performance often are not measured.

1. Can you think of instances where important aspects of performance are not measured?

2. What are ways you can compensate for this omission?

SUMMARY OF EFFECTIVE MEASUREMENT

In summary, measurement systems are most effective when they:

◇ Measure what's important and not just what's easy to measure

◇ Are developed with input from both the employees who will do the measuring and customers who use the end products or services

◇ Are regularly reviewed to see what measures need to be changed, added or discarded

◇ Use a limited number of measures

◇ Are simple to use and easy to interpret

◇ Emphasize identifying and understanding what works as well as what doesn't work

GUIDELINES FOR DEVELOPING PERFORMANCE MEASURES

Who Should Be Involved?

◇ *Top management.* What to measure is directly related to goals and key success factors, so top management should be involved in deciding, or at least in approving, what gets measured and how.

◇ *Middle and first level supervisors* who set goals and success factors for their own units similarly must decide, or at least approve, what is measured in their units.

◇ *Other employees* who have to do the measuring. They'll know what it makes sense to measure and how easy or difficult it will be to get the data. Also, if people participate in decisions on what and how to measure, they are more likely than nonparticipants to be committed to carrying out those decisions.

◇ *Other stakeholders* who will be affected by the results. These include other units within the company that your unit interacts with in carrying out work, and customers and others outside the company. Customers especially can provide valuable information on what aspects of performance they value and what their priorities are; for example, whether they value timeliness more than low cost, durability more than appearance of the product, and so on.

Worksheet

Ask the following questions.

1. What aspects of performance do you wish to measure—quality, quantity, cost, others?

_____

_____

_____

2. Prioritize the above. Are they critical to your business? Nice to have but not critical?

_____

_____

_____

3. What are measures of each of these? (Some will have multiple measures. Review the "What Usually Gets Measured" section earlier in this chapter for suggestions.)

_____

_____

_____

4. From #2 and #3, prepare a list of all the measures you'd like to track. Answer the following questions for each one.

- Is it really important to our business to have this measure?

- What would happen if we dropped it?

- Are we including any measures just because they're easy to get?

- Are there important aspects of performance we left off our list just because they're difficult to measure? If so, should we make a special effort to develop measures for them?

- Who will use the information we gather from these measures, and what will they do with it?

- Is this information likely to help us improve performance (or the blame on individuals)?

5. The above analysis may lead you to add or drop some measures on your list. Review the measures that remain, and for each one, determine:

- How the data will be collected—through a computer program, logbook, machine count or other?

- Who will collect the data—supervisors, workers, administrative clerks, others?

- How often data will be collected—daily, weekly, monthly or for each task as it's completed?

- Who will compile and report the results, and how frequently?

- Who will communicate the results? To whom?

- What is the process for making sure that results are acted on?

6. Decide at what intervals you will review measurement systems.

Chapter Six

PUTTING

THE

PIECES

TOGETHER

Now that you have worked through the major pieces of a new organization design, it's time to put them together, stand back and look at the whole.

We suggest you gather your notes—including any charts, descriptions and organized lists—from each of the preceding chapters. It's helpful to post organization charts and lists of issues so that you can see them all at once. If your organization is small to medium-sized, you may be able to create one organization chart that shows all the boxes and lines. If your organization is large, you may need to examine your design in sections.

IMPLEMENTING THE CHANGES

Having spent time, money and effort in designing your organization, it's important that you now pay equal attention to seeing that the new organization is well implemented. There are many fine publications that discuss the topic of implementing organizational change far more thoroughly than we can do here. (See the references included in this book.)

We will, however, briefly touch on three particularly important facets of implementation. These are *communication, impact analysis,* and *transition management.*

Communication

You are off to a head start if you have involved relevant stakeholders throughout the design process. This means there are people who will already understand some things about the design and hopefully have some degree of commitment to making it work. But it most likely wasn't possible to involve all the stakeholders all of the time. So the first important part of implementation is to communicate.

What to Communicate

The purpose of the communication is to describe the new organization, how it is different from the old and the reasons for the changes.

Employees will want to know how their jobs will be affected: if they'll be doing different work, reporting to a new supervisor, working with different people or transferred to a new location.

Labor unions, if you have them, will similarly want to know how their members will fare in the change, if work rules are to be altered or any other aspects of the labor union contract affected.

Customers will want to know if products and services will be different, if they'll be working with different contact people from your organization or if procedures for handling orders will change.

Others outside the organization who may be affected will want to know what impact the new organization has on them. These others might include shareholders, suppliers, banks, community groups, and so on.

How to Communicate

It's useful to have both written and face-to-face communications. A written communication provides a document that the recipient can refer to at will—while face-to-face settings, such as meetings, enable the audience to interact with the presenters.

Common ways of communicating a new organization design to employees include the following:

◇ An organizationwide meeting in which the new organization is presented to everyone at once. (In large organizations today, this is made possible through the use of modern technology like satellite broadcasts; questions from employees at remote locations are submitted by telephone.)

◇ A "cascading" series of meetings where each level of management describes the new organization to their employees.

◇ Written notices sent to all employees or posted on bulletin boards, on electronic mail, and so on.

To people outside the organization, methods of communication include:

◇ Newsletters or annual reports

◇ Individual meetings (for example, with major suppliers or customers), as appropriate

◇ Press conferences, shareholder meetings, and so on

No matter how you choose to communicate, it's important to give people the chance to raise questions and concerns and, if possible, have these addressed. In fact, this kind of two-way communication is critical throughout the entire implementation process.

Impact Analysis

Before implementing the new design, it's important to think through the impact any changes will have on other aspects of your organization—the "ripple effects." This is important in three ways. First, it helps you identify what needs to be done to implement the new organization. Second, it helps you anticipate and manage disruptions in the work that may occur during implementation. Third, it will uncover resistance or active opposition to the new design.

To arrive at a list of issues you'll need to resolve, consider holding a brainstorming session with people inside the organization and some of those outside the organization who are likely to be affected. In particular, if different steps of key business processes occur in different parts of the company, be sure to involve representatives of every step in your brainstorming session.

If you had earlier made a decision to design an "ideal" organization, leaving aside the needs and talents of existing employees, now is the time to consider how current employees will fit into the proposed organization—and whether the proposed design should be modified to accommodate your current work force, facilities or other resources.

There are many issues that generally come up in an impact analysis. Some of the major ones are:

- **Personnel.** Can the staffing needs of your proposed organization be filled with existing employees? Will there be new hires or layoffs? Will some people have to be transferred to other jobs, or other physical locations? Will training be needed for different job duties? Is morale likely to suffer? (It often does, especially when jobs are lost or changed.)

- **Labor Unions.** If you have unionized employees, will labor contract provisions be affected? If so, how will you negotiate with the unions?

- **Space and Equipment.** Will new or different office or plant space be required? New or different tools and equipment? New office technology, such as computers or telephones?

- **Costs.** What will be the costs of making these changes in terms of salaries, training, changes in space or equipment?

- **Productivity.** Will productivity be affected during the changeover? (It often dips when changes of any kind are made.) What arrangements will you make to monitor and minimize this effect?

- **Systems.** Will you need to develop new systems—for example, for job appraisals, compensation, management information, measuring performance?

- **Communication Channels.** Will customers, suppliers, regulators or other stakeholders have to communicate with your organization in different ways?

Presenting the Information

Once you've identified the issues, appoint a person or group to examine each issue or set of issues and make recommendations as to how to proceed. Their findings will be relevant to the implementation time schedule. Also, they may recommend that some parts of the proposed design be modified or postponed for consideration at another time.

Transition Management

Once an impact analysis is completed, you'll have an understanding of some of the things that need to be managed in making the transition to the new organization.

The more wide-ranging the changes you're planning to make, the more important it is to have a *transition plan.* This would lay out the steps involved in moving from the old to the new organization, who is responsible for doing what and the timing of each event.

In a large organizational change affecting many people, you may wish to appoint a *transition coordinator* or *transition manager* to oversee the changes and possibly have a *transition team* to assist this person. (Incidentally, in terms of organization design, this would be a "project team" with an assigned task of limited duration.)

This coordinator and team would help address questions such as:

◇ How is existing work to be handled while the organization is in transition?

◇ Do employees need guidance to close down their previous work assignments before moving to new assignments?

◇ Will old and new organizations coexist for a time, with the latter being phased in gradually? Or will there be an official "changeover day" with all changes being made at one time?

◇ How will you keep track of changes to make sure the new organization is actually implemented as planned? And to make sure that it is working as efficiently and effectively as you had anticipated?

KEY SUCCESS FACTORS AND DESIGN

The "ideal" design alternative for one key success factor might be quite different from the ideal alternative for another factor. Since trade-offs are inevitable, you may be able to organize around the most critical success factor and find other ways to ensure that your other success factors are addressed.

Different success factors may be operable at different times. Also, it is quite appropriate to respond to the needs of different parts of the organization in different ways. For example, an organization may have both a research and development (R&D) department and a manufacturing department with quite different success factors and correspondingly different design needs.

Key success factors for R&D may be to keep ahead of competitors technologically and build initiative and creativity in employees. The best design alternatives might, therefore, be a flat structure with broad spans of control. Employee commitment and broadly specified outcomes may be the best means of coordination and control.

On the other hand, the key success factor for manufacturing may be keeping production costs low. Thus, this department would probably want more centralized decision making, with standardization of both process and outcomes.

Table 6-1 on pages 134–135 lists examples of common success factors and indicates which aspects of organization design it is appropriate to consider for each. We'd like to stress that the design alternatives shown should be treated as a starting point only. It's important to refer to the full discussion in the relevant chapters to see under what conditions each alternative would work best, what the potential drawbacks are and what other alternatives may be better in your own situation.

REVIEW OF MAJOR ISSUES

Whatever the size of your organization, or however broad or narrow the scope of your design efforts, it will be helpful to think through the major issues one more time.

1. Do your organization's mission, goals and key success factors capture what your business is about and what you need to do to succeed? Do the business processes you've identified match your mission and goals?

The mission and goals of your organization define what you're trying to achieve, your basic direction. These, combined with your particular business situation, determine your key success factors—the things you must do to be successful. It's important to be clear about all three because the design of your organization can help or hinder you in achieving them.

Understanding your business processes helps you see where there are critical interdependencies in the work and the need for coordination.

2. Does the way you've divided up the work into units like divisions and departments support your business processes?

No matter how work is divided—whether by function, product, customer, and so on—the structure should help you carry out your business processes. For example, highly interdependent steps in each business process should be located close to each other so that coordination and control of those steps is easier.

3. Is your management structure appropriate for the control and coordination you need to carry out your business processes? Does it match the degree of independence, knowledge and skill your employees can exercise in doing their work?

You need enough levels of management to handle the tasks of coordinating and controlling work, but not so many that they get in the way of making effective and efficient use of your resources. Some decisions will need to be centralized, while others will serve customers and the success of your company better if they are decentralized.

TABLE 6-1. Key Success Factors and Organization Design

Key Success Factor	Design Alternatives to Consider
Efficiency—low costs of production	*Work structure:* Functional organization promotes economies of scale, having similar work done in same place. Business process teams lower costs of coordination across functions. *Management structure:* Centralized decision making can help control costs. *Coordination and Control:* All techniques could work. Think about standardized process, teams, employee commitment.
Effectiveness—understanding and responding to customers' needs	*Work structure:* Customer-based or business process teams. *Management structure:* Decentralized decision making, flat structure. *Coordination and control:* Employee commitment, teams, standardized outcomes.
Technological leadership	*Work structure:* Product-based or functional. *Management structure:* Decentralized decision making with respect to technological decisions. *Coordination and control:* Supervision with participating, delegating or coaching styles; broadly specified outcomes, employee commitment.
High quality work and products (accuracy, durability, etc.)	*Work structure:* Business process teams, functional or product-based. *Management structure:* Any could work. *Coordination and control:* Standardized process with measurement at interim steps in the work process, and standardized outcomes are commonly used. Teams, employee commitment and supervision can also work.

Fast turnaround or cycle time	*Work structure:* Business process teams.
	Management structure: Flat, decentralized decision making.
	Coordination and control: Teams, standardized outcomes, supervision.
Flexibility and efficiency in allocating resources	*Work structure:* Matrix.
	Management structure: Centralized decision making for companywide flexibility.
	Coordination and control: Any, but especially teams, employee commitment.
Employee initiative and creativity	*Work structure:* Business process and customer-based structures promote customer service. Product-based and functional promote new technology development.
	Management structure: Flat, broad spans of control, decentralized decision making.
	Coordination and control: Employee commitment, standardized outcomes.
Broadening employee skills	*Work structure:* Matrix, business process.
	Management structure: Flat, broad spans of control, decentralized decision making.
	Coordination and control: Standardized outcomes, teams, employee commitment.

Note: Treat these design alternatives as a starting point only. Please refer to the relevant chapters for a full discussion of their use and potential drawbacks.

4. Do the methods of control and coordination you have selected provide the right mix of reliance on employees to do the right thing and on managers to ensure that the right thing is done?

You will most likely use a mix of supervision and standardization to control and coordinate work. In addition, if your company is like many others today, you'll be increasingly exploring the use of teams and relying, to some extent at least, on employee commitment to make sure the right work is done the right way.

In general, it's a good idea to delegate to employees as much responsibility and authority as they can handle—or maybe just a tad more than they are comfortable with if you want them to develop more knowledge and initiative. (In the latter case, good management or team support should be available.)

Finally, it's important to keep track of performance through the use of appropriate measurement systems, and to use the results both to discover and correct the sources of poor performance and to discover and reward the sources of good performance.

IN CONCLUSION

The design of your organization is not carved in stone. Indeed, because organizations today face unprecedented competition and unpredictable markets, they need to be more finely attuned than ever to their customers and to changing business conditions.

The key to continued success is to have a firm-enough organizational structure to guide productive activity and provide stability, but also a flexible enough structure that you can change to meet the changing needs of your business environment. As the old saw goes, "the only constant is change." We all might as well develop the knowledge and skills to handle it.

There is no cut and dried formula for arriving at organization design decisions. Every alternative you choose will involve tradeoffs. You may, for example, want the high level of expertise a functional structure fosters, combined with the quick responsiveness to customers that is better served by a horizontal (business process) structure. The solution is to pick what you think is the best all-round alternative and find ways to make up for potential weaknesses in your choice. If you have thought through the "Points to Ponder" questions in this book, you may already have found ways to overcome or lessen the effects of many design drawbacks.

One cautionary note: It's important not to get carried away with all the latest management buzzwords and fads. While there is much value in many of the latest recipes for success, some involve "old wine in new bottles." The fundamental issues in structuring an organization remain very much the same as they have been for many decades.

We hope this book helps you make your choices and get good results from doing so.

REFERENCES

AND

FURTHER READING

CHAPTER 1

Davenport, Thomas H. *Process Innovation: Reengineering Work Through Information Technology.* Boston: Harvard Business School Press, 1993.

Delavigne, Kenneth T. and J. Daniel Robertson. *Deming's Profound Changes: When Will the Sleeping Giant Awake?* Englewood Cliffs, NJ: PTR Prentice-Hall, 1994.

Flanigan, Eileen M. and Jon Scott. *Process Improvement.* Menlo Park, CA: Crisp Publications, 1995.

Haines, Stephen G. *Successful Strategic Planning.* Menlo Park, CA: Crisp Publications, 1995.

Harrington, H. James. *Business Process Improvement.* New York: McGraw-Hill, 1991.

Latzko, William J. and David M. Saunders. *Four Days with Dr. Deming: A Strategy for Modern Methods of Management.* Reading, MA: Addison-Wesley, 1995.

Melan, Eugene H. *Process Management: Methods for Improving Products and Services.* New York: McGraw-Hill, 1992.

CHAPTER 2

Hammer, Michael and James Champy. *Reengineering the Corporation.* New York: HarperBusiness, 1993.

Hammer, Michael and Steven Stanton. *The Reengineering Revolution: A Handbook.* New York: HarperBusiness, 1995.

Ostroff, Frank and Doug Smith. "Blueprint for a Horizontal Organization," *Fortune,* May 18, 1992.

CHAPTER 3

Block, Peter. *Stewardship: Choosing Service Over Self-Interest.* San Francisco: Berrett-Koehler, 1993.

Champy, James. *Reengineering Management: The Mandate for New Leadership.* New York: HarperBusiness, 1995.

Drucker, Peter. *Management: Tasks, Responsibilities, Practices.* New York: HarperBusiness, 1974.

CHAPTER 4

Benfari, Robert. *Changing Your Management Style: How to Evaluate and Improve Your Own Performance.* New York: Lexington Books, 1995.

Haass, Richard N. *The Power to Persuade: How to Be Effective in Government, the Public Sector, and Any Unruly Organization.* Boston: Houghton-Mifflin, 1994.

Hersey, Paul and Ken Blanchard. *Management of Organizational Behavior* (Sixth Edition). Englewood Cliffs, NJ: Prentice-Hall, 1992.

Kouzes, James M. and Barry Z. Posner. *The Leadership Challenge*. San Francisco: Jossey-Bass, 1987.

Larson, Carl E. and Frank M. J. LaFasto. *TeamWork.* Newbury Park, CA: Sage Publications, 1989.

Packard, David. *The HP Way: How Bill Hewlett and I Built Our Company.* New York: HarperBusiness, 1995.

Torres, Cresencio and Jerry Spiegel. *Self-Directed Work Teams: A Primer.* San Diego: Pfeiffer & Co., 1990.

CHAPTER 6

Fossum, Lynn. *Understanding Organizational Change.* Los Altos, CA: Crisp Publications, 1989.

O'Toole, James. *Leading Change: Overcoming the Ideology of Comfort and the Tyranny of Custom.* San Francisco: Jossey-Bass, 1995.

Scott, Cynthia D. and Dennis T. Jaffe. *Managing Organizational Change.* Los Altos, CA: Crisp Publications, 1989.

GLOSSARY

Accountability The state of being held answerable for results.

Authority The right to make decisions about what others do and how they do it, how much money to spend on what, and so on.

Autonomy In a work setting, refers to having control over one's activities and relative freedom from supervision.

Business Process The sequence of tasks and activities that must be completed to provide a product or service to the customer.

Centralized/Decentralized How concentrated or dispersed the authority to make decisions is.

Chain of Command See *Management Hierarchy*

Commitment, Employee See *Employee Commitment*

Competitors, Competition People or companies outside the organization who seek to capture the same customers.

Control Making sure the right work is getting done in the right way, and instigating corrective action if expected results are not achieved.

Coordination Linking together the activities of individuals and/or organizational units to produce a desired outcome—for example, a product or service.

Core Business Process A business process that is directly related to the organization's mission.

Cross-Functional Team A team whose members represent different functions or units.

Culture, Corporate The set of shared attitudes, values and behaviors that characterize an organization.

Customer Anyone who uses the products or services of an organization. Usually called a client where professional services are provided—for example, by a lawyer or consultant. (In this book, we use the term *customer* to refer to anyone who receives goods or services from an organization.)

Customer-Based Structure A structure that forms units according to the characteristics or location of its customers or markets—for example, *California Division, Nevada Division, Men's Clothing Division, Women's Clothing Division.*

Decentralized See *Centralized/Decentralized*

Delegation of Authority The situation where a person with authority to make certain decisions formally transfers that authority to subordinates.

Division of Labor Separation of work into tasks that can be done by different people or organizational units.

Economies of Scale The savings obtained in cost and time when a large number of similar activities or products is processed at the same time, by the same equipment, in the same place or by the same people.

Effectiveness Getting desired results or doing what will meet the customers' needs.

Efficiency Accomplishing results with the least wasteful use of resources.

Employee In our usage, everyone who draws a paycheck from an organization. This term thus encompasses both managers and workers.

Employee Commitment Employee dedication to the success of the organization. Usually implies a strong belief in the values and goals of the organization.

Employee Involvement The practice of involving employees in solving problems and making decisions.

Environment, Business Political, economic and competitive conditions outside the organization that have an impact on the organization. These include major political or natural events; new technology; demographic shifts and the actions and attitudes of customers, governments, competitors, advocacy groups and community organizations.

First-Level Management The managers who directly supervise workers—the lowest level of management (also commonly called *first-level supervisor*).

Flat Structure An organization structure with relatively few levels from the highest management level to the worker level.

Flowcharting See *Workflow Charting*

Functional Structure A structure that has units formed according to major technical or professional function performed—for example, *Sales, Engineering.*

Goals Concrete results that the organization intends to achieve within a specified time period.

Headcount The number of employees in an organization's work force.

Hierarchy, Management See *Management Hierarchy*

Horizontal Structure A structure based on business process teams. It is called horizontal because the work units cut across traditional functions rather than relying on a vertical hierarchy to coordinate activity.

Hybrid Organization An organization that has a mix of structural forms. For example, it may be product-based at the highest level, with functional departments within each product division.

Impact Analysis   An analysis conducted prior to implementing an organizational change. Its purpose is to determine how the proposed new organization design will affect existing structures, systems, people and results.

Implementation   In connection with organization design, actually making the changes in the organization to reflect the new design.

Influence   The ability to affect what others do or believe, regardless of whether one has the authority to do so.

Informal Organization   Nonofficial procedures and channels of communication regularly used by employees.

Information Systems   Typically, computer-based systems to collect, organize and display information useful to the business.

Implementation   The process of putting into practice a plan, design, strategy or idea.

Inputs   Resources that are fed into a work process. These include the skills and knowledge of people, information, materials, and so on.

Interdependence   The extent to which two or more steps or tasks depend on each other. For example, the outcome of one step is the input for the next step, or a mistake made in one step will lead to flawed results in the next step.

Involvement, Employee   See *Employee Involvement*

Job   A relatively stable cluster of activities and responsibilities assigned to one person.

Key Success Factors   Something an organization must do well in order to be successful—for example, *keep costs low* or *respond quickly to customer requests.*

Management Hierarchy   The ordering of people and work in levels, one above the other. The people at each level supervise those in the level below them. The bottom level in an organization consists of workers, also sometimes called *individual contributors,* who do not supervise others.

Management Structure Reflects the way managers are distributed throughout the organization, in terms of the hierarchy or number of levels of management, spans of control and the centralization or decentralization of decision making.

Management Style The way that managers interact with people at lower levels in the organization—in particular, how much control the manager exerts or how much autonomy employees are permitted.

Manager Someone who is responsible for directing, coordinating and controlling the work.

Market The field of action where goods and services are bought and sold.

Matrix Structure A structure where individuals simultaneously report to two or more supervisors.

Measuring Performance The process of gathering information about outcomes produced by people or organizations.

Middle Management The levels of management between the top level (chief executive officer and those reporting directly to him/her) and the first-level managers who directly supervise workers.

Mission The ongoing purpose of an organization, or the reason it exists.

Motivation Something that causes a person to behave in a certain way. Positive motivational factors include rewards such as salary, interesting work, dedication to the company's success.

Noncore Process A work process that does not directly affect the organization's mission.

Organization Any collection of people or activities formed for a specific purpose. The purpose can be to make money, as with most business organizations, or to accomplish other purposes—such as charity, recreation, political action, education, worship and so on.

Organizational Chart A chart that displays how the work of an organization is divided up into "boxes" (divisions, departments, and so on) and who reports to whom (the "lines").

Organization Design Planning and fitting together the people and activities in an organization.

Outcomes The results of work activity, such as products and services. This term is often used interchangeably with *outputs* or *results.*

Performance Describes the results accomplished by an individual or organization, often in comparison with goals, targets or other criteria.

Performance Measurement See *Measuring Performance*

Power The ability to control the actions and decisions of others even if they resist.

Procedures Descriptions of how a task or activity is done, often written down in detail.

Process, Business See *Business Process*

Product-Based Structure A structure that forms units according to products or services delivered to customers—for example, *Refrigerator Division, Oven Division, Savings Accounts, Credit Card Accounts.*

Productivity The quantity of products and services delivered divided by the amount of resources (labor, capital, materials, equipment) used. (Total output divided by total input.) Also see *Efficiency*

Profit Center A division of an organization that is evaluated according to the profits it generates. Profit centers can generate their own revenues and make their own business decisions.

Profitability The extent to which revenues exceed costs.

Quality The extent to which goods or services meet or exceed expectations or standards.

Reengineering The process of completely rethinking and redesigning how an organization carries out its work.

Regulators Government agencies that impose rules and restrictions on organizations.

Reorganization Changing any component of an organization including its mission, goals, strategies and structures.

Resources People, money, materials, technology or anything else that helps the organization to produce its goods and services.

Restructuring Changing the structure of an organization: the way work is divided into units, number of levels of hierarchy, spans of control, and so on.

Rightsizing Adjusting work force size so there are the "right" (fewest necessary) number of people to carry out the work that must be done.

Self-Managing Teams Employee teams who have considerable authority to make decisions concerning the team and its work. These decisions include setting goals, deciding how to do the work, assigning work, allocating resources and selecting team members.

Semi-Autonomous Teams Another name for *Self-Managing Teams.*

Span of Control Refers to the number of people directly reporting to a manager or supervisor. If there are relatively few people, it is a narrow span of control; if relatively many, it is a broad span of control.

Stakeholder All those people or institutions who have an interest in an organization and who can influence its actions and success. Stakeholders include customers, employees, other units, shareholders, suppliers, and regulators.

Standardization Setting standards and criteria to make sure that events follow a predictable path and produce predictable outcomes. Organizations can standardize work *process, outcomes* of work and *inputs* to the work.

Strategy A plan for how the organization will carry out its mission and achieve its goals.

Structure, Organization Refers to the way that people and activities are clustered and relate to one another as shown on an organization chart. It includes the way work is divided into units like divisions and departments, the levels of hierarchy, spans of control, and centralization or decentralization of decision making.

Supervision The process of overseeing, coordinating and controlling the activities and outcomes of others.

Style, Management See *Management Style*

Subordinates Nonmanagement employees. We have generally used the term *workers* rather than subordinates.

Success Factors See *Key Success Factors*

Survey A set of questions, administered either verbally or through a written questionnaire, to customers, employees or others to gather information on attitudes, experiences with company products or practices and so on.

System A set of procedures pertaining to a certain function. For example, a compensation system would prescribe salary levels for different jobs, how salary increases are to be decided, and so on.

Tall Structure A structure with many supervisory levels from top management to the worker level.

Task A specific piece of work.

Team A group of employees who work together to accomplish a task.

Technology The scientific knowledge, methods, tools and equipment used to produce goods and services. The term *high technology* refers to the use of sophisticated electronic devices and methods.

Technology-Driven An organization, market, product or service that develops because of the technology that enables it to exist.

Total Quality Management (TQM) A movement promoting a collection of ideas and techniques that enables continuous improvement in work processes and the resulting products.

Transition In our usage, refers to the period of time when an organization is changing from its existing design to a new design.

Unit In our usage, any subdivision of an organization—for example, division, department, team.

Values Deeply held and enduring beliefs about what is good and desirable.

Workers In our usage, refers to employees who do not manage or supervise anyone. (Also referred to as *subordinates* or *individual contributors*.)

Workflow Charting Diagramming all the tasks in a work process to delineate the sequence of activities, the inputs to each task and the outputs generated.

ABOUT THE AUTHORS

Margaret Davis has advised more than 200 executives and managers on the design of their organizations. She was with Pacific Gas & Electric for 10 years, five as the director of the company's management consulting section. In addition, she has been a senior research sociologist at SRI International, researching the impact of organizations and government programs on families.

In 1984, Davis wrote a guide to organization design for PG&E officers and managers and revised this in 1993 with David Weckler. She has published numerous articles on her work and written a book on the effects of work on family life. Davis received her Ph.D. in sociology (formal organizations) from Stanford University where she spent two years in the organizations research training program.

David Weckler has a broad background in organization development, management consulting and work redesign. He has been a consultant to many organizations, including AT&T, General Motors, Stanford University and Pacific Gas & Electric. He has published articles and given presentations on high-commitment organizations, self-managed teams and work design.

Weckler earned his Ph.D. in psychology and completed post-doctoral studies in organizational behavior and research at Stanford University. He has also been an associate professor and founder/director of a graduate program in Industrial and organizational psychology.

He is currently a consultant in the Organizational Change Group, Western Region, of Development Dimensions, International (DDI). DDI is an international human resources and organizational change consulting firm headquartered in Pittsburgh, Pennsylvania.